W9-CRC-916

A BURST OF LIGHT
and Other Essays

Audre Lorde

Foreword by
Sonia Sanchez

ixia
PRESS

Mineola, New York

To that piece of
each of us which refuses
to be silent.

Bibliographical Note

This Ixia Press edition, first published in 2017, is an unabridged republication of the work originally published by Firebrand Books, Ithaca, New York, in 1988. A Foreword by Sonia Sanchez has been specially prepared for this edition.

International Standard Book Number

ISBN-13: 978-0-486-81899-3
ISBN-10: 0-486-81899-3

IXIA PRESS
An imprint of Dover Publications, Inc.

Manufactured in the United States by LSC Communications
81899301   2017
www.doverpublications.com/ixiapress

Acknowledgments

I wish to acknowledge with gratitude all the women whose loving feedback helped make the essay "A Burst of Light" happen. In particular, Frances Clayton, Blanche Cook, Clare Coss, Adrienne Rich, and Gloria Joseph; with special thanks to Judy D. Simmons of *Essence* magazine for her skilled and insightful editing, and Nancy K. Bereano of Firebrand Books for her patience and support.

Contents

Foreword

That time
we all heard it,
cool and clear …

Warning, in music-words
devout and large,
that we are each other's
harvest:
we are each other's
business:
we are each other's
magnitude and bond.

–*Paul Robeson* by Gwendolyn Brooks

My Dear Sister Audre,

It is today. Not yesterday. *Hoy ha llegado*—today has arrived. Sometimes I have gotten lost in this journey called today, where nothing moved, when I gathered up the country's hysteria, when I looked at the world's delirium, when I saw America try to disagree with its blood. But I always remembered your voice, feasting on love and intellect, across telephone wires as you talked, your voice a prayer in exile, pushing past the debris of human sacrifice.

A new century appeared, my dear Sister—a fragile bird caught in its past wing flow. This new century arrived and we saw death, generational death, peeling our skins down to our blood plasma.

And I asked you question after question, distracted by the scandal of billionaires accessorizing their flesh with newly minted coins. Where are we on this food chain of life to be eaten so easily century after century, decade after decade? Are these meditations of insane men and women from a takeout menu, imperializing our taste buds 'til we sweat, crouched junkies of an American dream, vomiting into the ears of our unborn fetuses? Are we like our ancestors, fated to end hanging from a morning sky of death?

I return to *A Burst of Light* for light. Communion. I need to remember the solitary earthquake of your breath, making us remember our blood.

Lo Purísimo: Your words explaining this American apartheid of 1986, still resounding in our 2017 ears. You remind us again how slow the economic process has been for the majority of African Americans in America and Africans on the continent. You remind us again how fast Black blood has been shed on both continents. We remember names we had forgotten: Eleanor Bumpers, a 66-year-old Black grandmother killed by two shotgun blasts from the NYPD during eviction proceedings; Allene Richardson, 64 years old, gunned down by a Detroit policeman; 10-year-old Clifford Glover shot in Queens by a policeman in front of his stepfather; 15-year-old Randy Evans's brains blown out while he sat on a stoop talking to a friend. We see that Black lives have never mattered to America, to Africa.

Lo Profundo: Sister Maya Angelou wrote about the privilege of being a Black woman. She said it was not a passive exercise; it required work that at times could be painful. Pain often accompanies privilege, she added. And your privilege of being a Black lesbian came with pain dancing in the eye of your pores. In your clarity about Black women uniting in spite of their pain, in spite of their sexual differences, we see the logic and power of all Black women, all queer women, *all* women, organizing, coming together in order to live. Survive. Be. Remember our humanity. Indeed: "Make God finally break the habit of being man."

Lo Purísimo: We hear you questioning your life. Days. Hours. The questions and answers you discovered as you began your journey with liver cancer. We hear the sound of bravery in your teeth. And we store in our blood the memory of your voice. Your genius, your words linking continents, making us broaden our minds.

Lo Profundo: Sister Grace Boggs said: "My revolution is to share my/our love, beauty and our history[herstory], experiences, successes and failures—of exits and entrances, to make *space for our souls.*"

In Japan it's said that the words of the soul reside in a spirit called *kotodama,* or the spirit of words, and that the act of speaking words has the power to change the world. Your words, my dear Sister, helped us to change the world. You rescued us from the tyranny of racism, sexism, homophobia, class and economic poverty . . . You. Prodigious singer. Of life and actions. And words . . .

> finally . . . to
> remember . . . you gave
> light to our eyes . . . . .

> In love/struggle/peace – Sister Sonia Sanchez
> June 8, 2017

Sadomasochism: Not About Condemnation

An Interview with Audre Lorde by Susan Leigh Star

Without a rigorous and consistent evaluation of what kind of a future we wish to create, and a scrupulous examination of the expressions of power we choose to incorporate into all our relationships including our most private ones, we are not progressing, but merely recasting our own characters in the same old weary drama. . . . S/M is not the sharing of power, it is merely a depressing replay of the old and destructive dominant/subordinate mode of human relating and one-sided power, which is even now grinding our earth and our human consciousness into dust.

—Audre Lorde[1]

1

I SPENT JUNE and July of 1980 in rural Vermont, an idyllic, green, vital world, alive in a short summer season. I teach there summers and winters. One afternoon, Sue (another teacher) and I lay sunbathing on a dock in the middle of a small pond. I suddenly imagined what it would be like to see someone dressed in black leather and chains, trotting through the meadow, as I am accustomed to seeing in my urban neighborhood in San Francisco. I started laughing as one of the parameters of the theater of sadomasochism became clear: it is about cities and a created culture, like punk rock, which is sustained by a particularly urban technology.

Later in the week, Sue and I drove over bumpy dirt roads far into the Northeast Kingdom, the most rural area of Vermont, to interview Audre Lorde. Again, I was struck by the incongruity of sitting in the radiant sunshine, with radiant Audre and Frances and Sue, listening to bobwhites and watching the haze lift far down in the valley, and the subject of our conversation seemed to belong to another world.

I include this description of our physical surroundings because it seems important to me to recognize that all conversations about sadomasochism take place in particular places and at particular historical times which ought to be noted and compared.

Leigh: How do you see the phenomenon of sadomasochism in the lesbian community?

Audre: Sadomasochism in the lesbian-feminist community cannot be seen as separate from the larger economic and social issues surrounding our communities. It *is* reflective of a whole social and economic trend of this country.

Sadly, sadomasochism feels comfortable to some people in this period of development. What is the nature of this allure? Why an emphasis on sadomasochism in the straight media? Sadomasochism is congruent with other developments going on in this country that have to do with dominance and submission, with disparate power—politically, culturally, and economically.

The attention that Samois* is getting is probably out of proportion to the representation of sadomasochism in the lesbian community. Because s/m is a theme in the dominant culture, an attempt to "reclaim" it rather than question it is an excuse not to look at the content of the behavior. For instance, "We are lesbians doing this extreme thing, and you're criticizing *us!*" Thus, sadomasochism is used to delegitimize lesbian-feminism, lesbianism, and feminism.

Leigh: So you're saying that the straight media both helps amplify the phenomenon within the lesbian community and that they focus on lesbians in particular as a way of not dealing with the larger implications and the very existence of the phenomenon in the world?

Audre: Yes. And because this power perspective is so much a part of the larger world, it is difficult to critique in isolation. As Erich Fromm once said, "The fact that millions of people take part in a delusion doesn't make it sane."

Leigh: What about the doctrine of "live and let live" and civil liberties issues?

---

* The San Francisco-based lesbian s/m organization.

Audre: I don't see that as the point. I'm not questioning anyone's right to live. I'm saying we must observe the implications of our lives. If what we are talking about is feminism, then the personal is political and we can subject everything in our lives to scrutiny. We have been nurtured in a sick, abnormal society, and we should be about the process of reclaiming ourselves as well as the terms of that society. This is complex. *I speak not about condemnation* but about recognizing what is happening and questioning what it means. I'm not willing to regiment *anyone's* life, but if we are to scrutinize our human relationships, we must be willing to scrutinize all aspects of those relationships. The subject of revolution is ourselves, is our lives.

Sadomasochism is an institutionalized celebration of dominant/subordinate relationships. And, it prepares us either to accept subordination or to enforce dominance. *Even in play,* to affirm that the exertion of power over powerlessness is erotic, is empowering, is to set the emotional and social stage for the continuation of that relationship, politically, socially, and economically.

Sadomasochism feeds the belief that domination is inevitable and legitimately enjoyable. It can be compared to the phenomenon of worshipping a godhead with two faces, and worshipping only the white part on the full moon and the black part on the dark of the moon, as if totally separate. But you cannot corral any aspect within your life, divorce its implications, whether it's what you eat for breakfast or how you say good-bye. This is what *integrity* means.

Leigh: That relates to two central arguments put forth by the women of Samois: that liberal tolerance is necessary in the realm of sexuality and that the *power over* part of the relationship is confined to the bedroom. I feel, as you do, that it is dangerous to try to cordon off such a vital part of our lives in this way.

Audre: If it is confined to the bedroom, then why was the Samois booklet (*What Color Is Your Handkerchief?: A Lesbian S/M Sexuality Reader*) printed? If it is not, then what does that mean? It is in the interest of a capitalist profit system for us to privatize much of our experience. In order to make integrated life choices, we must open the sluice gates in our lives, create emotional consistency. This is not to say that we act the same way, or do not change and grow, but that there is an underlying integrity that asserts itself in all of our actions. None of us is perfect, or born with that integrity, but we can work toward it as a goal.

The erotic weaves throughout our lives, and integrity is a basic condition that we aspire to. If we do not have the lessons of our journeys toward that condition, then we have nothing. From that life-vision, one is free to examine varying paths of behavior. But integrity has to be a basis for the journey.

Certain things in every society are defined as totally destructive. For instance, the old example of crying "fire" in a crowded theater. Liberalism allows pornography and has allowed wife beating as First Amendment rights. But this doesn't fit them into my life-vision, and they are both an immediate threat to my life.

The question I ask, over and over, is *who is profiting from this?* When sadomasochism gets presented on center stage as a conflict in the feminist movement, I ask, what conflicts are *not* being presented?

Leigh: How do you think sadomasochism starts? What are its roots?

Audre: In the superior/inferior mold which is inculcated within us at the deepest levels. The learned intolerance of differences.

Those involved with sadomasochism are acting out the intolerance of differences which we all learn: superiority and thereby the right to dominate. The conflict is supposedly self-limiting because it happens behind bedroom doors. Can this be so, when the erotic empowers, nourishes, and permeates all of our lives?

I ask myself, under close scrutiny, whether I am puritanical about this—and I have asked myself this very carefully—and the answer is no. I feel that we work toward making integrated life-decisions about the networks of our lives, and those decisions lead us to other decisions and commitments—certain ways of viewing the world, looking for change. If they don't lead us toward growth and change, we have nothing to build upon, no future.

Leigh: Do you think sadomasochism is different for gay men than for lesbians?

Audre: Who profits from lesbians beating each other? White men have been raised to believe that they're God; most gay white men are marginal in only one respect. Much of the gay white movement seeks to be included in the American dream and is angered when they do not receive the standard white male privileges, misnamed as "American democracy."

Often, white gay men are working *not* to change the system. This is one of the reasons why the gay male movement is as white as it is. Black gay men recognize, again by the facts of survival, that being Black, they are not going to be included in the same way. The Black/white gay male division is being examined and explored by some. Recently, for instance, there was a meeting of Third World lesbians and gays in Washington. It was recognized that there are things we do not share with white lesbians and gay men, as well as things that we do, and that clarification of goals is necessary between white gays and lesbians, and Third World gays and lesbians.

I see no essential battle between many gay men and the white male establishment. To be sure, there are gay men who do not view their oppressions as isolated, and who work for a future. But it is a matter of majority politics: many gay white males are being pulled by the same strings as other white men in this society. You do not get people to work against what they have identified as their basic self-interest.

Leigh: So one of the things that you're saying is that the politics of s/m are connected with the politics of the larger movements?

Audre: I do not believe that sexuality is separate from living. As a minority woman, I know dominance and subordination are not bedroom issues. In the same way that rape is not about sex, s/m is not about sex but about how we use power. If it were only about personal sexual exchange or private taste, why would it be presented as a political issue?

Leigh: I often feel that there's a kind of tyranny about the whole concept of *feelings,* as though, if you feel something then you must act on it.

Audre: You don't *feel* a tank or a war—you feel hate or love. Feelings are not wrong, but you are accountable for the behavior you use to satisfy those feelings.

Leigh: What about how Samois and other lesbian sadomasochists use the concept of power?

Audre: The s/m concept of "vanilla" sex is sex devoid of passion. They are saying that there can be no passion without unequal power. That feels very sad and lonely to me, and destructive. The linkage of passion to dominance/subordination is the prototype of the heterosexual image of male-female relationships, one which justifies pornography. Women are supposed to love being brutalized. This is also the prototypical justification of all relationships of oppression—that the subordinate one who is "different" enjoys the inferior position.

The gay male movement, for example, is invested in distinguishing between gay s/m pornography and heterosexual pornography. Gay men can allow themselves the luxury of not seeing the consequences. We, as women and as feminists, must scrutinize our actions and see what they imply, and upon what they are based.

As women, we have been trained to follow. We must look at the s/m phenomenon and educate ourselves, at the same time being aware of intricate manipulations from outside and within.

Leigh: How does this relate specifically to lesbian-feminism?

Audre: First, we must ask ourselves, is this whole question of s/m sex in the lesbian community perhaps being used to draw attention and energies away from other more pressing and immediately life-threatening issues facing us as women in this racist, conservative, and repressive period? A red herring? A smoke screen for provocateurs? Second, lesbian s/m is not about what you do in bed, just as lesbianism is not simply a sexual preference. For example, Barbara Smith's work on women-identified women, on "lesbian" experiences in Zora Hurston or Toni Morrison.[2] It is not who I sleep with that defines the quality of these acts, not what we do together, but what life-statements I am led to make as the nature and effect of my erotic relationships percolate throughout my life and my being. As a deep lode of our erotic lives and knowledge, how does our sexuality enrich us and empower our actions?

Notes

1. Audre Lorde, "Letter to the Editor," *Gay Community News* 7:37 (April 12, 1980), p. 4.
2. Barbara Smith, "Toward a Black Feminist Criticism," *Conditions Two* (October 1977), pp. 25–44.

I Am Your Sister:
Black Women Organizing Across Sexualities

WHENEVER I COME to Medgar Evers College I always feel a thrill of anticipation and delight because it feels like coming home, like talking to family, having a chance to speak about things that are very important to me with people who matter the most. And this is particularly true whenever I talk at the Women's Center. But, as with all families, we sometimes find it difficult to deal constructively with the genuine differences between us and to recognize that unity does not require that we be identical to each other. Black women are not one great vat of homogenized chocolate milk. We have many different faces, and we do not have to become each other in order to work together.

It is not easy for me to speak here with you as a Black Lesbian feminist, recognizing that some of the ways in which I identify myself make it difficult for you to hear me. But meeting across difference always requires mutual stretching, and until you *can* hear me as a

Black Lesbian feminist, our strengths will not be truly available to each other as Black women.

Because I feel it is urgent that we not waste each other's resources, that we recognize each sister on her own terms so that we may better work together toward our mutual survival, I speak here about heterosexism and homophobia, two grave barriers to organizing among Black women. And so that we have a common language between us, I would like to define some of the terms I use: *Heterosexism*—a belief in the inherent superiority of one form of loving over all others and thereby the right to dominance; *Homophobia*—a terror surrounding feelings of love for members of the same sex and thereby a hatred of those feelings in others.

In the 1960s, when liberal white people decided that they didn't want to appear racist, they wore dashikis, and danced Black, and ate Black, and even married Black, but they did not want to feel Black or think Black, so they never even questioned the textures of their daily living (why should flesh-colored Band-Aids always be pink?) and then they wondered, "Why are those Black folks always taking offense so easily at the least little thing? Some of our best friends are Black. . . ."

Well, it is not necessary for some of your best friends to be Lesbian, although some of them probably are, no doubt. But it is necessary for you to stop oppressing me through false judgment. I do not want you to ignore my identity, nor do I want you to make it an insurmountable barrier between our sharing of strengths.

When I say I am a Black feminist, I mean I recognize that my power as well as my primary oppressions come as a result of my

Blackness as well as my womanness, and therefore my struggles on both these fronts are inseparable.

When I say I am a Black Lesbian, I mean I am a woman whose primary focus of loving, physical as well as emotional, is directed to women. It does not mean I hate men. Far from it. The harshest attacks I have ever heard against Black men come from those women who are intimately bound to them and cannot free themselves from a subservient and silent position. I would never presume to speak about Black men the way I have heard some of my straight sisters talk about the men they are attached to. And of course that concerns me, because it reflects a situation of noncommunication in the heterosexual Black community that is far more truly threatening than the existence of Black Lesbians.

What does this have to do with Black women organizing?

I have heard it said—usually behind my back—that Black Lesbians are not normal. But what is normal in this deranged society by which we are all trapped? I remember, and so do many of you, when being Black was considered *not normal,* when they talked about us in whispers, tried to paint us, lynch us, bleach us, ignore us, pretend we did not exist. We called that racism.

I have heard it said that Black Lesbians are a threat to the Black family. But when 50 percent of children born to Black women are born out of wedlock, and 30 percent of all Black families are headed by women without husbands, we need to broaden and redefine what we mean by *family.*

I have heard it said that Black Lesbians will mean the death of the race. Yet Black Lesbians bear children in exactly the same way other women bear children, and a Lesbian household is simply another kind of family. Ask my son and daughter.

The terror of Black Lesbians is buried in that deep inner place where we have been taught to fear all difference—to kill it or ignore it. Be assured: loving women is not a communicable disease. You don't catch it like the common cold. Yet the one accusation that seems to render even the most vocal straight Black woman totally silent and ineffective is the suggestion that she might be a Black Lesbian.

If someone says you're Russian and you know you're not, you don't collapse into stunned silence. Even if someone calls you a bigamist, or a childbeater, and you know you're not, you don't crumple into bits. You say it's not true and keep on printing the posters. But let anyone, particularly a Black man, accuse a straight Black woman of being a Black *Lesbian,* and right away that sister becomes immobilized, as if that is the most horrible thing she could be, and must at all costs be proven false. That is homophobia. It is a waste of woman energy, and it puts a terrible weapon into the hands of your enemies to be used against you to silence you, to keep you docile and in line. It also serves to keep us isolated and apart.

I have heard it said that Black Lesbians are not political, that we have not been and are not involved in the struggles of Black people. But when I taught Black and Puerto Rican students writing at City College in the SEEK program in the sixties I was a Black Lesbian. I was a Black Lesbian when I helped organize and fight for the Black Studies Department of John Jay College. And because I was fifteen years younger then and less sure of myself, at one crucial moment I yielded to pressures that said I should step back for a Black man even though I knew him to be a serious error of choice, and I did, and he was. But I was a Black Lesbian then.

When my girlfriends and I went out in the car one July 4th night after fireworks with cans of white spray paint and our kids asleep in the back seat, one of us staying behind to keep the motor running and watch the kids while the other two worked our way down the suburban New Jersey street, spraying white paint over the black jockey statues, and their little red jackets, too, we were Black Lesbians.

When I drove through the Mississippi delta to Jackson in 1968 with a group of Black students from Tougaloo, another car full of redneck kids trying to bump us off the road all the way back into town, I was a Black Lesbian.

When I weaned my daughter in 1963 to go to Washington in August to work in the coffee tents along with Lena Horne, making coffee for the marshalls because that was what most Black women did in the 1963 March on Washington, I was a Black Lesbian.

When I taught a poetry workshop at Tougaloo, a small Black college in Mississippi, where white rowdies shot up the edge of campus every night, and I felt the joy of seeing young Black poets find their voices and power through words in our mutual growth, I was a Black Lesbian. And there are strong Black poets today who date their growth and awareness from those workshops.

When Yoli and I cooked curried chicken and beans and rice and took our extra blankets and pillows up the hill to the striking students occupying buildings at City College in 1969, demanding open admissions and the right to an education, I was a Black Lesbian. When I walked through the midnight hallways of Lehman College that same year, carrying Midol and Kotex pads for the young Black radical women taking part in the action, and we tried to persuade them that their place in the revolution was not ten paces behind Black men, that spreading their legs to the guys on the tables in the cafeteria was not a revolutionary act no matter what the brothers said, I was a Black Lesbian. When I picketed for Welfare Mothers' Rights, and against the enforced sterilization of young Black girls, when I fought institutionalized racism in the New York City schools, I was a Black Lesbian.

But you did not know it because we did not identify ourselves, so now you can say that Black Lesbians and Gay men have nothing to do with the struggles of the Black Nation.

And I am not alone.

When you read the words of Langston Hughes you are reading the words of a Black Gay man. When you read the words of Alice Dunbar-Nelson and Angelina Weld Grimké, poets of the Harlem Renaissance, you are reading the words of Black Lesbians. When you listen to the life-affirming voices of Bessie Smith and Ma Rainey, you are hearing Black Lesbian women. When you see the plays and read the words of Lorraine Hansberry, you are reading the words of a woman who loved women deeply.

Today, Lesbians and Gay men are some of the most active and engaged members of Art Against Apartheid, a group which is making visible and immediate our cultural responsibilities against the tragedy of South Africa. We have organizations such as the National Coalition of Black Lesbians and Gays, Dykes Against Racism Everywhere, and Men of All Colors Together, all of which are committed to and engaged in antiracist activity.

Homophobia and heterosexism mean you allow yourselves to be robbed of the sisterhood and strength of Black Lesbian women because you are afraid of being called a Lesbian yourself. Yet we share so many concerns as Black women, so much work to be done. The urgency of the destruction of our Black children and the theft of young Black minds are joint urgencies. Black children shot down or doped up on the streets of our cities are priorities for all of us. The fact of Black women's blood flowing with grim regularity in the streets and living rooms of Black communities is not a Black Lesbian rumor. It is sad statistical truth. The fact that there is widening and dangerous lack of communication around our differences between Black women and men is not a Black Lesbian plot. It is a reality that is starkly clarified as we see our young people becoming more and more uncaring of each other. Young Black boys believing that they can define their manhood between a sixth-grade girl's legs, growing up believing that Black women and girls are the fitting target for their justifiable furies rather than the racist structures grinding us all into dust, these are not Black Lesbian myths. These are sad realities of Black communities today and of immediate concern to us all. We cannot afford to waste each other's energies in our common battles.

What does homophobia mean? It means that high-powered Black women are told it is not safe to attend a Conference on the Status of Women in Nairobi simply because we are Lesbians. It means that in a political action, you rob yourselves of the vital insight and energies of political women such as Betty Powell and Barbara Smith and Gwendolyn Rogers and Raymina Mays and Robin Christian and Yvonne Flowers. It means another instance of the divide-and-conquer routine.

How do we organize around our differences, neither denying them nor blowing them up out of proportion?

The first step is an effort of will on your part. Try to remember to keep certain facts in mind. Black Lesbians are not apolitical. We have been a part of every freedom struggle within this country. Black Lesbians are not a threat to the Black family. Many of us have families of our own. We are not white, and we are not a disease. We are women who love women. This does not mean we are going to assault your daughters in an alley on Nostrand Avenue. It does not mean we are about to attack you if we pay you a compliment on your dress. It does not mean we only think about sex, any more than you only think about sex.

Even if you *do* believe any of these stereotypes about Black Lesbians, begin to practice *acting* like you don't believe them. Just as racist stereotypes are the problem of the white people who believe them, so also are homophobic stereotypes the problem of the heterosexuals who believe them. In other words, those stereotypes are yours to solve, not mine, and they are a terrible and wasteful barrier to our working together. I am not your enemy. We do not have to become each other's unique experiences and insights in order to share what we have learned through our particular battles for survival as Black women....

There was a poster in the 1960s that was very popular: HE'S NOT BLACK, HE'S MY BROTHER! It used to infuriate me because it implied that the two were mutually exclusive—*he* couldn't be both brother and Black. Well, I do not want to be tolerated, nor misnamed. I want to be recognized.

I am a Black Lesbian, and I *am* your sister.

Apartheid U.S.A.

NEW YORK CITY, 1985. The high sign that rules this summer is increasing fragmentation. I am filled with a sense of urgency and dread: dread at the apparently random waves of assaults against people and institutions closest to me; urgency to unearth the connections between these assaults. Those connections lurk beneath the newspaper reports of teargassed funeral processions in Tembisa and the charred remains of Baldwin Hills, California, a flourishing Black neighborhood leveled by arson.

I sit before the typewriter for days and nothing comes. It feels as if underlining these assaults, lining them up one after the other and looking at them squarely might give them an unbearable power. Yet I know exactly the opposite is true—no matter how difficult it may be to look at the realities of our lives, it is there that we will find the strength to change them. And to suppress any truth is to give it power beyond endurance.

As I write these words I am listening to the United Nations Special Session considering the "state of emergency" in South Africa, their euphemism for the suspension of human rights for Blacks, which is the response of the Pretoria regime to the increasingly spontaneous eruptions in Black townships across that country. These outbursts against apartheid have greatly increased in the last eleven months since a new South African constitution further solidified the exclusion of the twenty-two million Black majority from the South African political process. These outbreaks, however severely curtailed by the South African police and military, are beginning to accomplish what Oliver Tambo, head of the African National Congress, hoped for in his call to make South Africa under apartheid "ungovernable."

So much Black blood has been shed upon that land, I thought, and so much more will fall. But blood will tell, and now the blood is speaking. Has it finally started? What some of us prayed and worked and believed would—must—happen, wondering when, because so few of us here in America even seemed to know what was going on in South Africa, nor cared to hear. The connections have not been made, and they must be if African-Americans are to articulate our power in the struggle against a worldwide escalation of forces aligned against people of Color the world over: institutionalized racism grown more and more aggressive in the service of shrinking profit-oriented economies.

And who would have thought we'd live to see the day when Black South Africa took center stage on the world platform? As Ellen Kuzwayo, Black South African writer, would say, this is where we are right now in the world's story. . . . Perhaps this is how Europe felt in the fall of 1939, on the brink. I remember that Sunday of December 7, 1941 and the chill certainty that some threat which hovered on my six-year-old horizon had finally been made real and frontal. August 6, 1945. Hiroshima. My father's tears—I had never seen him cry before and at first I thought it was sweat—a forty-six-year-old Black man in his vigor, yet only seven years away from death by overwork. He said, "Humanity can now destroy itself," and he wept. That's how it feels, except this time we know we're on the winning side. South Africa *will* be free, I thought, beneath the clatter of my waiting typewriter and the sonorous tones of the United Nations broadcast, the U.S. delegate, along with the one from Great Britain, talking their rot about what "we" have done for Black South Africa.

South Africa. Eighty-seven percent of the people, Black, occupy 13 percent of the land. Thirteen percent of the people, white, own 85 percent of the land. White South Africa has the highest standard of living of any nation in the world including the United States yet half the Black children born in South Africa die before they reach the age of five. Every thirty minutes, six Black children starve to death in South Africa. In response to questions about apartheid from a white U.S. reporter, a white South African reporter retorts, "You have solved the problem of your indigenous people—we are solving ours. You called them Indians, didn't you?" Apartheid—South Africa's Final Solution patterned after Nazi Germany's genocidal plan for European Jews.

Every year over 500 million American dollars flow into the white South African death machine. How many of those dollars do you control as you sit reading this? Where do you bank? Buy your gas? What pressure can you bring to bear upon companies doing business in South Africa? Five hundred million dollars a year. Divestment. The withdrawal of American financial support from

South Africa. Those who counter that divestment would mean additional suffering for Black South Africans are either cynical or misguided or unaware of the extent to which Black South Africans suffer every day of their lives. For any South African to even discuss divestment in South Africa is considered an act of treason against the state.

Do you even know which companies your money supports that do business in South Africa? You won't find that information in the *New York Times* or the *San Francisco Chronicle* or *GQ*. But you can obtain that information and more from the African National Congress Weekly News Briefings ($15 a year) from ANC, 801 Second Avenue, New York, NY 10017, or from the American Committee on Africa, 198 Broadway, New York, NY 10038.

We are Black Lesbians and Gays, fighting many battles for survival. We are also citizens of the most powerful country in the world, a country which stands upon the wrong side of every liberation struggle on earth. African-Americans control 200 billion dollars in buying power annually. As African-Americans we must learn to use our power, to establish the connections instantly between consistent patterns of slaughter of Black children and youth in the roads of Sebokeng and Soweto in the name of law and order in Johannesburg, and white America's not-so-silent applause for the smiling white vigilante who coolly guns down four Black youths in the New York City subway. Or the white policemen guarding the store of a Middle Eastern shopkeeper who had killed three Black children in Brooklyn in a dispute over one can of Coca-Cola. The multicorporate financial connections are a matter of record; it is the emotional ones which must become inescapable for each of us. We are members of an international community of people of Color, and must see our struggles as connected within that light.

Made more arrogant daily by the connivance of the U.S. dollar and the encouragement of the U.S. policy of constructive engagement, South African police jail and murder six-year-old children, kick twelve-year-old Johannes to death in front of his garden, leave nine-year-old Joyce bleeding to death on her granny's floor. Decades of these actions are finally escalating into the world's consciousness.

How long will it take to escalate into our consciousness as Black people that this is *us,* that it is only a matter of location and progression of time and intensity from the molotov cocktails that were hurled into the brush in Los Angeles, starting the conflagration that burned out well-to-do Black Baldwin Hills—fifty-three homes gone, three lives lost—to government sanctioned segregation and violence. In California, U.S.A., the Aryan Brotherhood, the Posse Commitatus, and other white racist and anti-Semitic survivalist groups flourish rampant and poisonous, fertilized by a secretly sympathetic law enforcement team.

Eleanor Bumpurs, sixty-six, Black grandmother, evicted from her Bronx Housing Authority apartment with two fatal shotgun blasts from New York City Housing police.

Allene Richardson, sixty-four, gunned down in her Detroit apartment house hallway by a policewoman after she was locked out of her apartment and a neighbor called the police to help her get back in.

It is ten years since a policeman shot ten-year-old Clifford Glover early one Saturday morning in front of his father in Queens, New York; eight years Thanksgiving Day since another white cop walked up to Randy Evans while he sat on his stoop talking with friends and blew his fifteen-year-old brains out. Temporary insanity, said the jury that acquitted that policeman.

Countless others since then—Seattle, New Orleans, Dallas. Yvonne Smallwood, a young Black woman arguing her husband's traffic ticket, kicked to death by police in Manhattan. Our dead line our dreams, their deaths becoming more and more commonplace.

How does a system bent upon our ultimate destruction make the unacceptable gradually tolerable? Observe closely, look around, read the Black press. How do you get a population to accept the denial of the most rudimentary freedoms this country is supposed to be about to over 12 percent of its population? And we know that Black Americans are only the beginning, just as the moves against Black Lesbians and Gays are only the beginning within our communities.

In 1947, within my memory, apartheid was not the state policy of South Africa, but the supposedly far-out dream of the Afrikaner Broederbond. Living conditions of Black South Africans, although bad, were not yet governed by policies of institutional genocide. Blacks owned land, attended schools.

With the 1948 election of the Afrikaner white-supremacy advocate Malik, and the implementation of apartheid, the step-by-step attack upon Black existence was accelerated with the dismantling of any human rights as they pertained to Black people. Now, white South Africans who protest are being jailed and brutalized and blown up, also. Once liberal English-speaking white South Africans had to be conned into accepting this dismantling, lulled long enough for the apparatus which was to ensure all white privileged survival to be cemented into place by H. Verwoerd, its architect and later South African Prime Minister.

Now Johannesburg, city of gold, sits literally upon a mountain of gold and Black blood.

After a Sharpeville, why not a Soweto? After a Michael Stewart, young Black artist beaten to death by New York City transit police, why not a Bernard Goetz? After a New York Eight Plus, why not a Philadelphia, where the Black mayor allows a white police chief to bomb a houseful of Black people into submission, killing eleven people and burning down a whole Black neighborhood to do it. Firemen refused to douse the flames. Five of those killed were children. Police pinned them down with gunfire when the occupants sought to escape the flames, making sure these Black people died. Because they were dirty and Black and obnoxious and Black and arrogant and Black and poor and Black and Black and Black and Black. And the Mayor who allowed this to happen says he accepts full responsibility, and he is Black, too. How are we persuaded to participate in our own destruction by maintaining our silences? How is the American public persuaded to accept as natural the fact that at a time when prolonged negotiations can effect the release of hostages in the Middle East or terminate an armed confrontation with police outside a white survivalist encampment, a mayor of an American city can order an incendiary device dropped on a house with five children in it and police pin down the occupants until they perish? Yes, African-Americans can still walk the streets of America without passbooks—for the time being.

In October 1984, 500 agents of the Joint Terrorists Task Force (see what your taxes are paying for?) rounded up eight middle-income Black radicals whose only crime seems to be their insistence upon their right to dissent, to call themselves Marxist-Leninists, and to question the oppressive nature of this U.S. society. They are currently imprisoned, and being tried in a Grand Jury proceeding that reads like the Star Chamber reports or the Spanish Inquisition. Twenty-two months of round-the-clock surveillance has so far not provided any evidence at all that these Black men and women, some grandmothers, were terrorists. I am reminded of the Johannesburg courts filled with cases brought against Black clericals and salesgirls accused of reading a book or wearing a T-shirt or listening to music thought to be sympathetic to the African National Congress. Two years hard labor for pamphlets discovered in an office desk drawer.

How is the systematic erosion of freedoms gradually accomplished? What kind of gradual erosion of our status as United States citizens will Black people be persuaded first to ignore and then to accept?

In Louisville, Kentucky, a Workmen's Compensation ruling awards $231 weekly disability payments to a thirty-nine-year-old sanitation supervisor, white, for a mental breakdown he says he suffered as a result of having to work with Black people.

A peaceful, licensed march to the Haitian Embassy in New York to protest living conditions on that island, and the imprisonment of three priests, is set upon by New York City mounted police and trained attack dogs. Sixteen people are injured, including women and children, and one man, struck in the head by hooves, may lose his eye. The next day, no major newspaper or TV news station carries a report of the incident, except for Black media.

In New York, the self-confessed and convicted white ex-G.I. killer of at least six Black men in New York City and Buffalo is quietly released from jail after less than one year, on a technicality. He had been sentenced to life for three of the murders and never tried on the others. White men attack three Black transit workers in Brooklyn, stomping one to death. Of the three who are tried for murder, two are sentenced to less than one year in prison and one goes scot-free.

So the message is clear: stock in Black human life in the U.S.A., never high, is plunging rapidly in the sight of white American complacencies. But as African-Americans we cannot afford to play that market; it is our lives and the lives of our children that are at stake.

The political and social flavor of the African-American position in the 1980s feels in particular aspects to be analogous to occurrences in the Black South African communities of the 1950s, the period of the postwar construction of the apparati of apartheid, reaction, and suppression. Reaction in a large, manipulated, and oppressed population, particularly one where minimal material possessions allow a spurious comparison for the better to one's neighbors, is always slow in coming, preceded as it so often is by the preoccupation of energies in having to cope daily with worsening symptoms of threatened physical survival.

There has recently been increased discussion among African-Americans concerning crime and social breakdown within our communities, signaled in urban areas by highly visible groups of unemployed Black youths, already hopeless and distrustful of their or their elders' abilities to connect with any meaningful future. Our young Black people are being sacrificed to a society's determination to destroy whomever it no longer needs for cheap labor or cannon fodder.

No one in the U.S. government will say openly now that apartheid in South Africa is good, or that the advancing technocracy in this country is making a large underprivileged pool of cheap labor increasingly unnecessary. No one actually says that Black people are more frequently seen as expendable in this economy, but nonetheless the nation that plans to finance Star Wars in space and run shuttle flights to the moon cannot seem to remedy Black teenage unemployment. Because it does not wish to remedy it. Better to wipe them out, blow them away. African-Americans are increasingly superfluous to a shrinking economy. A different stage exists in South Africa where a cheap labor pool of Blacks is still pivotal to the economy. But the maintenance of the two systems is closely related, and they are both guided primarily by the needs of a white marketplace. Of course no one in the United States government will openly defend apartheid—they don't have to. Just support it by empty rhetorical slaps on the wrist and solid financial investments, all the time honoring South African orders for arms, nuclear technology, and sophisticated computerized riot-control mechanisms. The bully boys stick together.

I remember stories in the 1960s about the roving bands of homeless and predatory *tsotsis,* disenchanted and furious Black youths roaming the evening streets of Sharpeville and Soweto and other Black townships.

The fact that African-Americans can still move about relatively freely, do not yet have to carry passbooks or battle an officially named policy of apartheid, should not delude us for a minute about the disturbing similarities of the Black situation in each one of these profit-oriented economies. We examine these similarities so that we can more effectively devise mutually supportive strategies for action, at the same time as we remain acutely aware of our differences. Like the volcano, which is one form of extreme earth-change, in any revolutionary process there is a period of intensification and a period of explosion. We must become familiar with the requirements and symptoms of each period, and use the differences between them to our mutual advantage, learning and supporting each other's battles. African-Americans can wield the relative power of our dollars—for better or worse. We have the ability to affect South Africa where it lives, financially, through our support of divestment for companies doing business in South Africa. Black South Africans have the base of their own land upon which they operate. We lack that as African-Americans, suffer the rootlessness of a "hyphenated" people. But within those differences, we can join together to effect a future the world has not yet conceived, let alone seen.

For no matter what liberal commitment to human rights is mouthed in international circles by the U.S. government, we know it will not move beyond its investments in South Africa unless we make it unprofitable to invest there. For it is economic divestment, not moral sanction, that South Africa fears most. No one will free us but ourselves, here nor there. So our survivals are not separate, even though the terms under which we struggle differ. African-Americans are bound to the Black struggle in South Africa by politics as well as blood. As Malcolm X observed more than twenty years ago, a militant, free Africa is a necessity to the dignity of African-American identity.

The mendacity of the U.S. Ambassador to the United Nations, as he recited all the "help" this country has given to Black South Africans, is matched only by the cynicism of the South African president who self-righteously condemns the spontaneous violence against Black collaborators in the Black townships, calling that the reason for the current state of emergency. Of course, it is the picture of Blacks killing a Black that is flashed over and over across the white world's TV screens, not the images of white South African police firing into groups of Black schoolchildren, imprisoning six-year-olds, driving over Black schoolgirls. And I think about my feelings concerning that Black mayor of Philadelphia, and about Clarence Pendleton, Black man, Reagan-appointed head of the Federal Civil Rights Commission and mouthpiece of corruption, saying to young students at Cornell University, "The economic pie is just too small for everyone to have a fair share, and that's not the function of civil rights." Eventually institutional racism becomes a question of power and privilege rather than merely color, which then serves as a subterfuge.

The connections between Africans and African-Americans, African-Europeans, African-Asians, is real, however dimly seen at times, and we all need to examine without sentimentality or stereotype what the injection of Africanness into the socio-political consciousness of the world could mean. We need to join our differences and articulate our particular strengths in the service of our mutual survivals, and against the desperate backlash which attempts to keep that Africanness from altering the very bases of current world power and privilege.

Turning the Beat Around:
Lesbian Parenting 1986

THESE DAYS IT seems like everywhere I turn somebody is either having a baby or talking about having a baby, and on one level that feels quite benign because I love babies. At the same time, I can't help asking myself what it means in terms of where we are as a country, as well as where we are as people of Color within a white racist system. And when infants begin to appear with noticeable regularity within the Gay and Lesbian community, I find this occurrence even more worthy of close and unsentimental scrutiny.

We are Lesbians and Gays of Color surviving in a country that defines human—when it concerns itself with the question at all—as straight and white. We are Gays and Lesbians of Color at a time in that country's history when its domestic and international policies, as well as its posture toward those developing nations with which we share heritage, are so reactionary that self-preservation demands we involve ourselves actively in those policies and postures. And we must have some input and effect upon those policies if we are ever to take a responsible place within the international community of peoples of Color, a human community which includes two-thirds of the world's population. It is a time when the increase in conservatism upon every front affecting our lives as people of Color is oppressively obvious, from the recent appointment of a Supreme Court Chief Justice in flagrant disregard of his history of racial intolerance, to the largely unprotested rise in racial stereotypes and demeaning images saturating our popular media—radio, television, videos, movies, music.

We are Gays and Lesbians of Color at a time when the advent of a new and uncontrolled disease has carved wrenching inroads into the ranks of our comrades, our lovers, our friends. And the connection between these two facts—the rise in social and political conservatism and the appearance of what has become known in the general public's mind as the *gay* disease, AIDS—has not been sufficiently scrutinized. But we certainly see their unholy wedding in the increase of sanctioned and self-righteous acts of heterosexism and homophobia, from queer-bashing in our streets to the legal invasion of our bedrooms. Should we miss these connections between racism and homophobia, we are also asked to believe that this monstrously convenient disease—and I use *convenient* here in the sense of *convenient for extermination*—originated spontaneously and mysteriously in Africa. Yet, for all the public hysteria surrounding AIDS, almost nothing is heard of the growing incidence of CAIDS—along the Mexican border, in the Near East and in the other areas of industrial imperialism. Chemically Acquired Immune Deficiency Syndrome is an industrial disease caused by prolonged exposure to trichloroethylene. TCE is a chemical in wholesale use in the electronic sweatshops of the world, where workers are primarily people of Color, in Malaysia, Sri Lanka, the Philippines, and Mexico.

It is a time when we, Lesbians and Gays of Color, cannot ignore our position as citizens of a country that stands on the wrong side of every liberation struggle on this globe; a country that publicly condones and connives with the most vicious and systematic program for genocide since Nazi Germany—apartheid South Africa.

How do we raise children to deal with these realities? For if we do not, we only disarm them, send them out into the jaws of the dragon unprepared. If we raise our children in the absence of an accurate picture of the world as we know it, then we blunt their most effective weapons for survival and growth, as well as their motivation for social change.

We are Gays and Lesbians of Color in a time when race-war is being fought in a small Idaho town, Coeur D'Alene. It is a time when the lynching of two Black people in California within twenty miles of each other is called nonracial and coincidental by the local media. One of the two victims was a Black Gay man, Timothy Lee; the other was a Black woman reporter investigating his death, Jacqueline Peters.

It is a time when local and national funds for day care and other programs which offer help to poor and working-class families are being cut, a time when even the definition of family is growing more and more restrictive.

But we are having babies! And I say, thank the goddess. As members of ethnic and racial communities historically under siege, every Gay and Lesbian of Color knows deep down inside that the question of children is not merely an academic one, nor do our children represent a theoretical hold upon some vague immortality. Our parents are examples of survival as a living pursuit, and no matter how different from them we may now find ourselves, we have built their example into our definitions of self—which is why we can be here, naming ourselves. We know that all our work upon this planet is not going to be done in our lifetimes, and maybe not even in our children's lifetimes. But if we do what we came to do, our children will carry it on through their own living. And if we can keep this earth spinning and remain upon it long enough, the future belongs to us and our children because we are fashioning it with a vision rooted in human possibility and growth, a vision that does not shrivel before adversity.

There are those who say the urge to have children is a reaction to encroaching despair, a last desperate outcry before the leap into the void. I disagree. I believe that raising children is one way of participating in the future, in social change. On the other hand, it would be dangerous as well as sentimental to think that childrearing alone is enough to bring about a livable future in the absence of any definition of that future. For unless we develop some cohesive vision of that world in which we hope these children will participate, and some sense of our own responsibilities in the shaping of that world, we will only raise new performers in the master's sorry drama.

So what does this all have to do with Lesbian parenting? Well, when I talk about mothering, I do so with an urgency born of my consciousness as a Lesbian and a Black African Caribbean American woman staked out in white racist sexist homophobic America.

I gave birth to two children. I have a daughter and a son. The memory of their childhood years, storms and all, remains a joy to me. Those years were the most chaotic as well as the most creative of my life. Raising two children together with my lover, Frances, balancing the intricacies of relationship within that four-person interracial family, taught me invaluable measurements for my self, my capacities, my real agendas. It gave me tangible and sometimes painful lessons about difference, about power, and about purpose.

We were a Black and a white Lesbian in our forties, raising two Black children. Making do was not going to be a safe way to live our lives, nor was pretense, nor euphemism. *Lesbian* is a name for women who love each other. *Black* means of African ancestry. Our lives would never be simple. We had to learn and to teach what works while we lived, always, with a cautionary awareness of the social forces aligned against us—at the same time there was laundry to be done, dental appointments to be kept, and no you can't watch cartoons because we think they rot your feelings and we pay the electricity.

I knew, for example, that the rage I felt and kept carefully under lock and key would one day be matched by a similar rage in my children: the rage of Black survival within the daily trivializations of white racism. I had to discover ways to own and use that rage if I was to teach them how to own and use theirs, so that we did not wind up torturing ourselves by turning our rage against each other. It was not restraint I had to learn, but ways to use my rage to fuel actions, actions that could alter the very circumstances of oppression feeding my rage.

Screaming at my daughter's childish banter instead of standing up to a racist bus driver was misplacing my anger, making her its innocent victim. Getting a migraine headache instead of injecting my Black woman's voice into the smug whiteness of a Women's Studies meeting was swallowing that anger, turning it against myself. Neither one of these actions offered solutions I wanted to give my children for dealing with relationships or racism. Learning to recognize and label my angers, and to put them where they belonged in some effective way, became crucial—not only for my own survival, but also for my children's. So that when I was justifiably angry with one of them—and no one short of sainthood can live around growing children and not get angry at one time or another—I could express the anger appropriate to the situation and not have that anger magnified and distorted by all my other unexpressed and unused furies. I was not always successful in achieving that distinction, but trying kept me conscious of the difference.

If I could not learn to handle my anger, how could I expect the children to learn to handle theirs in some constructive way—not deny it or hide it or self-destruct upon it? As a Black Lesbian mother I came to realize I could not afford the energy drains of denial and still be open to my own growth. And if we do not grow with our children, they cannot learn.

That was a long and sometimes arduous journey toward self-possession. And that journey was sweetened by an increasing ability to stretch far beyond what I had previously thought possible—in understanding, in seeing common events in a new perspective, in trusting my own perceptions. It was an exciting journey, sweetened also by the sounds of their laughter in the street and the endearing beauty of the bodies of children sleeping. My daughter and my son made issues of survival daily questions, the answers to which had to be scrutinized as well as practiced. And what our children learned about using their own power and difference within our family, I hope they will someday use to save the world. I can hope for no less. I know that I am constantly learning from them. Still.

Like getting used to looking up instead of down. How looking up all the time gives you a slight ache in the back of the neck. Jonathan, at seventeen, asking, "Hey Ma, how come you never hit us until we were bigger'n you?" At that moment realizing I guess I never hit my kids when they were little for the same reason my father never hit me: because we were afraid that our rage at the world in which we lived might leak out to contaminate and destroy someone we loved. But my father never learned to express his anger beyond imaginary conversations behind closed doors. Instead, he stoppered it, denying me his image, and he died of inchoate rage at fifty-one. My mother, on the other hand, would beat me until she wept from weariness. But it was not me, the overly rambunctious child, who sold her rotting food and spat upon her and her children in the street.

Frances and I wanted the children to know who we were and who they were, and that we were proud of them and of ourselves, and we hoped they would be proud of themselves and of us, too. But I remember Beth's fifteen-year-old angry coolness: "You think just because you're lesbians you're so different from the rest of them, but you're not, you're just like all the other parents. . . ." Then she launched into a fairly accurate record of our disciplines, our demands, our errors.

What I remember most of all now is that we were not just like all the other parents. Our family was not just like all the other families. That did not keep us from being a family any more than our being Lesbians kept Frances and me from being parents. But we did not have to be just like all the rest in order to be valid. We were an interracial Lesbian family with radical parents in the most conservative borough of New York City. Exploring the meaning of those differences kept us all stretching and learning, and we used that exploration to get us from Friday to Thursday, from toothache through homework to who was going to babysit when we both worked late and did Frances go to PTA meetings.

There are certain basic requirements of any child—food, clothing, shelter, love. So what makes our children different? We do. Gays and Lesbians of Color are different because we are embattled by reason of our sexuality and our Color, and if there is any lesson we must teach our children, it is that difference is a creative force for change, that survival and struggle for the future is not a theoretical issue. It is the very texture of our lives, just as revolution is the texture of the lives of the children who stuff their pockets with stones in Soweto and quickstep all the way to Johannesburg to fall in the streets from tear gas and rubber bullets in front of Anglo-American Corporation. Those children did not choose to die little heroes. They did not ask their mothers and fathers for permission to run in the streets and die. They do it because somewhere their parents gave them an example of what can be paid for survival, and these children carry on the same work by redefining their roles in an inhuman environment.

The children of Lesbians of Color did not choose their Color nor their mamas. But these are the facts of their lives, and the power as well as the peril of these realities must not be hidden from them as they seek self-definition.

And yes, sometimes our daughter and son did pay a price for our insisting upon the articulation of our differences—political, racial, sexual. That is difficult for me to say, because it hurts to raise your children knowing they may be sacrificed to your vision, your beliefs. But as children of Color, Lesbian parents or no, our children are programmed to be sacrifices to the vision of white racist profit-oriented sexist homophobic America, and that we cannot allow. So if we must raise our children to be warriors rather than cannon fodder, at least let us be very clear in what war we are fighting and what inevitable shape victory will wear. Then our children will choose their own battles.

Lesbians and Gays of Color and the children of Lesbians and Gays of Color are in the forefront of every struggle for human dignity in this country today, and that is not by accident. At the same time, we must remember when they are children that they are children, and need love, protection, and direction. From the beginning, Frances and I tried to teach the children that they each had a right to define herself and himself and to feel his own and her own feelings. They also had to take responsibility for the actions which arose out of those feelings. In order to do this teaching, we had to make sure that Beth and Jonathan had access to information from which to form those definitions—true information, no matter how uncomfortable it might be for us. We also had to provide them with sufficient space within which to feel anger, fear, rebellion, joy.

We were very lucky to have the love and support of other Lesbians, most of whom did not have children of their own, but who loved us and our son and daughter. That support was particularly important at those times when some apparently insurmountable breach left us feeling isolated and alone as Lesbian parents. Another source of support and connection came from other Black women who were raising children alone. Even so, there were times when it seemed to Frances and me that we would not survive neighborhood disapproval, a double case of chickenpox, or escalating teenage rebellion. It is really scary when your children take what they have learned about self-assertion and nonviolent power and decide to test it in confrontations with you. But that is a necessary part of learning themselves, and the primary question is, have they learned to use it well?

Our daughter and son are in their twenties now. They are both warriors, and the battlefields shift: the war is the same. It stretches from the brothels of Southeast Asia to the blood-ridden alleys of Capetown to the incinerated Lesbian in Berlin to Michael Stewart's purloined eyes and grandmother Eleanor Bumpurs shot dead in the projects of New York. It stretches from the classroom where our daughter teaches Black and Latino third graders to chant, "I am somebody beautiful," to the college campus where our son replaced the Stars and Stripes with the flag of South Africa to protest his school's refusal to divest. They are in the process of choosing their own weapons, and no doubt some of those weapons will feel completely alien to me. Yet I trust them, deeply, because they were raised to be their own woman, their own man, in struggle, and in the service of all of our futures.

A Burst of Light:
Living with Cancer

though we may land here there is no other landing
to choose our meaning we must make it new.

—Muriel Rukeyser

Introduction

THE YEAR I *became fifty felt like a great coming together for me. I was very proud of having made it for half a century, and in my own style. "Time for a change," I thought, "I wonder how I'm going to live the next half."*

On February 1st, two weeks before my fiftieth birthday, I was told by my doctor that I had liver cancer, metastasized from the breast cancer for which I had had a mastectomy six years before.

At first I did not believe it. I continued with my previously planned teaching trip to Europe. As I grew steadily sicker in Berlin, I received medical information about homeopathic alternatives to surgery, which strengthened my decision to maintain some control over my life for as long as possible. I believe that decision has prolonged my life, together

*with the loving energies of women who supported me in that decision
and in the work which gives that life shape.*

*The struggle with cancer now informs all my days, but it is only
another face of that continuing battle for self-determination and survival that Black women fight daily, often in triumph. The following
excerpts are from journals kept during my first three years of living
with cancer.*

~

January 15, 1984
NEW YORK CITY

I've just returned from three days in Washington, D.C. It was an
extraordinary reading. The second evening spent with the Sapphires
Sapphos was like 2001 Space Odyssey time—the past dreaming the
future blooming real and tasty into the present, now. During our evening together, I felt the love and admiration of other Black women
in a way I had not before—a web woven between us of the uses to
which my work has been put.

The Sapphires Sapphos are a group of Lesbians of Color who had
invited me to a special dinner at their regular monthly meeting. It
was held at the Clubhouse, a cozy wooden building at the back of a
city lot.

Coming in out of the D.C. winter storm felt like walking into an
embrace. The roaring fireplace, the low-beamed wooden room filled
with beautiful Black and Brown women, a table laden with delicious
foods so obviously cooked with love. There was sweet potato pie,
rice and red beans, black beans and rice, pigeon peas and rice, beans

and pimentos, spaghetti with Swedish meatballs, codfish and ackee, spinach noodles with clam sauce, five-bean salad, fish salad, and other salads of different combinations.

On gaily decorated trays and platters, a profusion of carefully prepared dishes waited proudly: steamed fish and fried fish and fish pâté, cornbread and succulent collard greens, stir-fry vegetables with ginger and tree-ears, startling and deliciously sensual. There was roti and almond bread, Jamaican harddough bread and sweet rolls, johnnycake and sourdough biscuits. And the punch! A cut-glass punchbowl filled with cassis and mineral water with a blessing of rum, fresh fruit floating seductively on top.

The whole spread reflected a dreamlike fullness of women sharing color and food and warmth and light—*Zami* come true. It filled me with pleasure that such a space could finally come to pass on an icy Tuesday evening in Washington, D.C., and I said so. Majote from Haiti looked exactly like Ginger, and we danced the night down.

~

January 19, 1984
NEW YORK CITY

I watched the movie *King* on TV tonight, and it brought those days of 1968 vividly back to me—the hope and the pain and the fury and the horror coming so close upon the possibility of change, a bare month after I'd left the Black student poets and my first meeting with Frances, at Tougaloo College in Mississippi. That night at Carnegie Hall when the Tougaloo Choir sang with Duke Ellington. A wealth of promise, of the student singers with their beautiful young Black faces, believing.

I was there to cover the concert for the Jackson, Mississippi, *Clarion Star Ledger.* "What the world needs now is love," they sang. Halfway through the song, the Master of Ceremonies interrupted to say that Dr. Martin Luther King had just been shot. "What the world needs now is love," they sang, tears lining their faces on stage catching the light, tears rolling down Mr. Honeywell's cheeks. "What the world needs now is love," they sang, his dark rhythmic arms directing the voices through all their weeping. And Dr. King is dead dead dead.

While I watched this movie I was also thinking about the course of my own life, the paths I feel bound for inside myself, the way of life that feels most real to me. And I wonder what I may be risking as I become more and more committed to telling whatever truth comes across my eyes my tongue my pen—no matter how difficult—the world as I see it, people as I feel them. And I wonder what I will have to pay someday for that privilege, and in whose coin? Will those forces which serve non-life in the name of power and profit kill me too, or merely dismember me in the eyes of whoever can use what I do?

When I stand in the radiance of a place like the Sapphires Sapphos dinner, with the elegant food and abundance of love and beautiful dark women, when I stand in that moment of sweetness, I sometimes become almost afraid. Afraid of their warmth and loving, as if that same loving warmth might doom me. I know this is not so, but it can feel like it. As if so long as I remained too different from my own time and surroundings I was safe, if terribly lonely. But now that I am becoming less lonely and more loved, I am also becoming more visible, and therefore more vulnerable. Malcolm saying to Martin in the film, "I love you Martin, and we are both dead men."

Audre Lorde

February 9, 1984
NEW YORK CITY

So. No doubt about where we are in the world's story. It has just cost $32,000 to complete a government-commissioned study that purports to show there is no rampant hunger in the U.S.A. I wonder if they realize *rampant* means *aggressive*.

So. The starving old women who used to sit in broken-down rooming houses waiting for a welfare check now lie under park benches and eat out of garbage bins. "I only eat fruit," she mumbled, rummaging through the refuse bin behind Gristede's supermarket, while her gnarled Black hands carefully cut away the rotted parts of a cantaloupe with a plastic Burger King knife.

~

February 18, 1984
OHIO

How does it *feel*, Ms. L., to be a fifty-year-old Black woman who is still bleeding! Cheers to the years! Doing what I like to do best.

Last night I gave a talk to the Black students at the University about coming to see ourselves as part of an international community of people of Color, how we must train ourselves to question what our Blackness—our Africanness—can mean on the world stage. And how as members of that international community, we must assume responsibility for our actions, or lack of action, as Americans. Otherwise, no matter how relative that power might be, we are yielding it up to the opposition to be used against us, and against the forces for liberation around the world. For instance, what are our responsibilities as educated Black women toward the land-rights struggles of other people of Color here and abroad?

I want to write down everything I know about being afraid, but I'd probably never have enough time to write anything else. Afraid is a country where they issue us passports at birth and hope we never seek citizenship in any other country. The face of afraid keeps changing constantly, and I can count on that change. I need to travel light and fast, and there's a lot of baggage I'm going to have to leave behind me. Jettison cargo.

~

February 19, 1984
NEW YORK CITY

Last night at Blanche and Clare's house was a celebration of my first fifty years. Liz Maybank called—such a wonderful gift to hear her voice across all these years since she helped care for my children. Black Women's Survival 101. I've had many teachers.

Forever is too long to think about. But the future has always been so real to me. Still is. Chances are I don't have liver cancer. No matter what they say. Chances are. That's good. That's bad. Either way I'm a hostage. So what's new?

Coming to terms with the sadness and the fury. And the curiosity.

~

March 18, 1984
EN ROUTE TO ST. CROIX, VIRGIN ISLANDS

I've written nothing of the intensity with which I've lived the last few weeks. The hepatologist who tried to frighten me into an immediate

45

liver biopsy without even listening to my objections and questions. Seeing the growth in my liver on the CAT scan, doing a face-off with death, again. Not again, just escalated. This mass in my liver is not a primary liver tumor, so if it is malignant, it's most likely metastasized breast cancer. Not curable. Arrestable, not curable. This is a very bad dream, and I'm the only person who can wake myself up. I had a talk before I left with Peter, my breast surgeon. He says that if it is liver cancer, with the standard treatments—surgery, radiation, and chemotherapy—we're talking four or five years at best. Without treatment, he says, maybe three or four.

In other words, western medicine doesn't have a very impressive track record with cancer metastasized to the liver.

In the light of those facts, and from all the reading I've been doing these past weeks (thank the goddess for Barnes & Noble's Medical Section), I've made up my mind not to have a liver biopsy. It feels like the only reasonable decision for me. I'm asymptomatic now except for a vicious gallbladder. And I can placate her. There are too many things I'm determined to do that I haven't done yet. Finish the poem "Outlines." See what Europe's all about. Make Deotha Chamber's story live.

If I have this biopsy and it is malignant, then a whole course of action will be established simply by their intrusion into the suspect site. Yet if this tumor is malignant, I want as much good time as possible, and their treatments aren't going to make a hell of a lot of difference in terms of extended time. But they'll make a hell of a lot of difference in terms of my general condition and how I live my life.

On the other hand, if this is benign, I believe surgical intervention into fatty tissue of any kind can start the malignant process in what otherwise might remain benign for a long time. I've been down that road before.

I've decided this is a chance I have to take. If this were another breast tumor, I'd go for surgery again, because the organ comes off. But with the tie-in between estrogens, fat cells, and malignancies I've been reading about, cutting into my liver seems to me to be too much of a risk for too little return in terms of time. And it might be benign, some little aberrant joke between my liver and the universe.

Twenty-two hours of most days I don't believe I have liver cancer. Most days. Those other two hours of the day are pure hell, and there's so much work I have to do in my head in those two hours, too, through all the terror and uncertainties.

I wish I knew a doctor I could really trust to talk it all over with. Am I making the right decision? I know I have to listen to my body. If there's one thing I've learned from all the work I've done since my mastectomy, it's that I must listen keenly to the messages my body sends. But sometimes they are contradictory.

Dear goddess! Face-up again against the renewal of vows. Do not let me die a coward, mother. Nor forget how to sing. Nor forget song is a part of mourning as light is a part of sun.

~

March 22, 1984
EN ROUTE TO NEW YORK CITY

This was a good trip. Good connections with the Sojourner Sisters and other women in St. Croix. And I finally taught myself to relax in water, swimming about under the sun in Gloria's pool to the sound of Donna Summers blowing across the bright water, "State of Independence," and the coconut tree singing along in the gentle tradewinds.

There was a poetry reading last night at the library, with a wide range of age and ability among the poets, but the audience was very responsive. It reminded me again of how important poetry can be in the life of an ordinary Black community when that poetry is really the poetry of the lives of the people who make up that community.

I suspect I shall have to concentrate upon how painful it is to think about death all the time.

In the spring of 1984, I spent three months in Berlin conducting a course in Black American women poets and a poetry workshop in English for German students. One of my aims for this trip was to meet Black German women. I'd been told there were quite a few in Berlin, but I had been unable to obtain much information about them in New York.

~

May 23, 1984
BERLIN, WEST GERMANY

Who are they, the German women of the Diaspora? Where do our paths intersect as women of Color—beyond the details of our particular oppressions, although certainly not outside the reference of those details? And where do our paths diverge? Most important, what can we learn from our connected differences that will be useful to us both, Afro-German and Afro-American?

Afro-German. The women say they've never heard that term used before.

I asked one of my Black students how she'd thought about herself growing up. "The nicest thing they ever called us was 'war baby,'" she said. But the existence of most Black Germans has nothing to do with the Second World War, and, in fact, predates it by many decades. I have Black German women in my class who trace their Afro-German heritage back to the 1890s.

For me, Afro-German means the shining faces of Katerina and Mai in animated conversation about their fathers' homelands, the comparisons, joys, disappointments. It means my pleasure at seeing another Black woman walk into my classroom, her reticence slowly giving way as she explores a new self-awareness, gains a new way of thinking about herself in relation to other Black women.

"I've never thought of Afro-German as a positive concept before," she said, speaking out of the pain of having to live a difference that has no name; speaking out of the growing power self-scrutiny has forged from that difference.

I am excited by these women, by their blossoming sense of identity as they're beginning to say in one way or another, "Let us be ourselves now as we define us. We are not a figment of your imagination or an exotic answer to your desires. We are not some button on the pocket of your longing." I can see these women as a growing force for international change, in concert with other Afro-Europeans, Afro-Asians, Afro-Americans.

We are the hyphenated people of the Diaspora whose self-defined identities are no longer shameful secrets in the countries of our origin, but rather declarations of strength and solidarity. We are an increasingly united front from which the world has not yet heard.

June 1, 1984
BERLIN

My classes are exciting and exhausting. Black women are hearing about them and their number is increasing.

I can't eat cooked food and I am getting sicker. My liver is so swollen I can feel it under my ribs. I've lost almost fifty pounds. That's a switch, worrying about losing weight. My friend Dagmar, who teaches here, has given me the name of a homeopathic doctor specializing in the treatment of cancer, and I've made an appointment to see her when I come back from the Feminist Bookfair in London next week. She's an anthroposophic doctor, and they believe in surgery only as a last resort.

In spite of all this, I'm doing good work here. I'm certainly enjoying life in Berlin, sick or not. The city itself is very different from what I'd expected. It is lively and beautiful, but its past is never very far away, at least not for me. The silence about Jews is absolutely deafening, chilling. There is only one memorial in the whole city and it is to the Resistance. At the entrance is a huge grey urn with the sign, "This urn contains earth from German concentration camps." It is such a euphemistic evasion of responsibility and an invitation to amnesia for the children that it's no wonder my students act like Nazism was a bad dream not to be remembered.

There is a lot of networking going on here among women, collectives and work enterprises as well as political initiatives, and a very active women's cultural scene. I may be too thin, but I can still dance!

June 7, 1984
BERLIN

Dr. Rosenberg agrees with my decision not to have a biopsy, but she has said I must do something quickly to strengthen my bodily defenses. She's recommended I begin Iscador injections three times weekly.

Iscador is a biological made from mistletoe which strengthens the natural immune system, and works against the growth of malignant cells. I've started the injections, along with two other herbals that stimulate liver function. I feel less weak.

I am listening to what fear teaches. I will never be gone. I am a scar, a report from the frontlines, a talisman, a resurrection. A rough place on the chin of complacency. "What are you getting so upset about, anyway?" a student asked in class, "You're not Jewish!"

So what if I am afraid? Of stepping out into the morning? Of dying? Of unleashing the damned gall where hatred swims like a tadpole waiting to swell into the arms of war? And what does that war teach when the bruised leavings jump an insurmountable wall where the glorious Berlin chestnuts and orange poppies hide detection wires that spray bullets which kill?

My poems are filled with blood these days because the future is so bloody. When the blood of four-year-old children runs unremarked through the alleys of Soweto, how can I pretend that sweetness is anything more than armor and ammunition in an on-going war?

I am saving my life by using my life in the service of what must be done. Tonight as I listened to the ANC speakers from South Africa at the Third World People's Center here, I was filled with a sense of self-answering necessity, of commitment as a survival weapon. Our battles are inseparable. Every person I have ever been must be actively enlisted in those battles, as well as in the battle to save my life.

~

June 9, 1984
BERLIN

At the poetry reading in Zurich this weekend, I found it so much easier to discuss racism than to talk about *The Cancer Journals*. Chemical plants between Zurich and Basel have been implicated in a definite rise in breast cancer in this region, and women wanted to discuss this. I talked as honestly as I could, but it was really hard. Their questions presume a clarity I no longer have.

It was great to have Gloria there to help field all those questions about racism. For the first time in Europe, I felt I was not alone but answering as one of a group of Black women— not just Audre Lorde!

I am cultivating every iota of my energies to do battle with the possibility of liver cancer. At the same time, I am discovering how furious and resistant some pieces of me are, as well as how terrified.

In this loneliest of places, I examine every decision I make within the light of what I've learned about myself and that self-destructiveness implanted inside of me by racism and sexism and the circumstances of my life as a Black woman.

Mother why were we armed to fight
with cloud wreathed swords and javelins of dust?

Survival isn't some theory operating in a vacuum. It's a matter of my everyday living and making decisions.

How do I hold faith with sun in a sunless place? It is so hard not to counter this despair with a refusal to see. But I have to stay open and filtering no matter what's coming at me, because that arms me in a particularly Black woman's way. When I'm open, I'm also less despairing. The more clearly I see what I'm up against, the more able I am to fight this process going on in my body that they're calling liver cancer. And I am determined to fight it even when I am not sure of the terms of the battle nor the face of victory. I just know I must not surrender my body to others unless I completely understand and agree with what they think should be done to it. I've got to look at all of my options carefully, even the ones I find distasteful. I know I can broaden the definition of winning to the point where I can't lose.

~

June 10, 1984
BERLIN

Dr. Rosenberg is honest, straightforward, and pretty discouraging. I don't know what I'd do without Dagmar there to translate all her grim pronouncements for me. She thinks it's liver cancer, too, but she respects my decision against surgery. I mustn't let my unwillingness to accept this diagnosis interfere with getting help. Whatever it is, this seems to be working.

We all have to die at least once. Making that death useful would be winning for me. I wasn't supposed to exist anyway, not in any meaningful way in this fucked-up whiteboys' world. I want desperately to live, and I'm ready to fight for that living even if I die shortly. Just writing those words down snaps every thing I want to do into a neon clarity. This European trip and the Afro-German women, the Sister Outsider collective in Holland, Gloria's great idea of starting an organization that can be a connection between us and South African women. For the first time I really feel that my writing has a substance and stature that will survive me.

I have done good work. I see it in the letters that come to me about *Sister Outsider,* I see it in the use the women here give the poetry and the prose. But first and last I am a poet. I've worked very hard for that approach to living inside myself, and everything I do, I hope, reflects that view of life, even the ways I must move now in order to save my life.

I have done good work. There is a hell of a lot more I have to do. And sitting here tonight in this lovely green park in Berlin, dusk approaching and the walking willows leaning over the edge of the pool caressing each other's fingers, birds birds birds singing under and over the frogs, and the smell of new-mown grass enveloping my sad pen, I feel I still have enough moxie to do it all, on whatever terms I'm dealt, timely or not. Enough moxie to chew the whole world up and spit it out in bite-sized pieces, useful and warm and wet and delectable because they came out of my mouth.

$\sim$

June 17, 1984
BERLIN

I am feeling more like an Audre I recognize, thank the goddess for Dr. Rosenberg, and for Dagmar for introducing me to her.

I've been reading Christa Wolf's *The Search for Christa T.,* and finding it very difficult. At first I couldn't grapple with it because it was just too painful to read about a woman dying. Dagmar and a number of the women here in Berlin say the author and I should meet. But now that I'm finished I don't know if I want to meet the woman who wrote it. There is so much pain there that is so far from being felt in any way I recognize or can use, that it makes me very uncomfortable. I feel speechless.

But there is one part of the book that really spoke to me. In Chapter 5, she talks about a mistaken urge to laugh at one's younger self's belief in paradise, in miracles. Each one of us who survives, she says, at least once in our lifetime, at some crucial and inescapable moment, has had to absolutely believe in the impossible. Of course, it occurs to me to ask myself if that's what I'm doing right now, believing in the impossible by refusing a biopsy.

It's been very reassuring to find a medical doctor who agrees with my view of the dangers involved. And I certainly don't reject nondamaging treatment, which is why I'm taking these shots, even though I hate giving myself injections. But that's a small price balanced against the possibility of cancer.

~

June 20, 1984
BERLIN

I didn't go to London because I loved bookfairs, but because the idea of the First International Feminist Bookfair excited me, and in particular, I wanted to make contact with the Black feminists of England. Well, the fact remains: the First International Feminist

Bookfair was a monstrosity of racism, and this racism coated and distorted much of what was good, creative, and visionary about such a fair. The white women organizers' defensiveness to any question of where the Black women were is rooted in that tiresome white guilt that serves neither us nor them. It reminded me of those old tacky battles of the seventies in the States: a Black woman would suggest that if white women wished to be truly feminist, they would have to examine and alter some of their actions vis-à-vis women of Color. And this discussion would immediately be perceived as an attack upon their very essence. So wasteful and destructive.

I think the organizers of the Bookfair really believed that by inviting foreign Black women they were absolving themselves of any fault in ignoring input from local Black women. But we should be able to learn from our errors. They totally objectified *all* Black women by not dealing with the Black women of the London community. Now if anything is to be learned from that whole experience, it should be so that the *next* International Feminist Bookfair does not repeat those errors. And there must be another. But we don't get *there* from *here* by ignoring the mud in between those two positions. If the white women's movement does not learn from its errors, like any other movement, it will die by them. When I stood up for my first reading to a packed house with no Black women's faces, after I'd gotten letter after letter from Black British women asking when was I coming to England, that was the kiss-off. I knew immediately what was up, and the rest is history.

Of course, I was accused of "brutalizing" the organizers by simply asking why Black women were absent. And if my yelling and "jumping up and down" got dirty looks and made white women cry and say all kinds of outrageous nonsense about me, I know it also reinforced other Black women's perceptions about racism here in the women's movement, and contributed to further solidarity among Black women of different communities.

Feminism must be on the cutting edge of real social change if it is to survive as a movement in any particular country. Whatever the core problems are for the people of that country must also be the core problems addressed by women, for we do not exist in a vacuum. We are anchored in our own place and time, looking out and beyond to the future we are creating, and we are part of communities that interact. To pretend otherwise is ridiculous. While we fortify ourselves with visions of the future, we must arm ourselves with accurate perceptions of the barriers between us and that future.

~

June 21, 1984
BERLIN

Rather than siphoning off energies in vain attempts to connect with women who refuse to deal with their own history or ours, Black women need to choose the areas where that energy can be most effective. Who are we? What are the ways in which we do not see each other? And how can we better operate together as a united front even while we explore our differences? Rather than keep yelling at white women's gates, we need to look at our own needs and start giving top priority to satisfying those needs in the service of our joint tasks. How do we deal across our differences of community, time, place, and history? In other words, how do we learn to love each other while we are embattled on so many fronts? I hope for an International Conference of Black Feminists, asking some of these questions of definition of women from Amsterdam, Melbourne, the South Pacific, Kentucky, New York and London, all of whom call ourselves Black feminists and all of whom have different strengths.

To paraphrase June Jordan, we are the women we want to become.

~

August 1, 1984
NEW YORK CITY

Saints be praised! The new CAT scan is unchanged. The tumor has not grown, which means either Iscador is working or the tumor is not malignant! I feel relieved, vindicated, and hopeful. The pain in my middle is gone, as long as I don't eat very much and stick to fruits and veggies. That's livable. I feel like a second chance, for true! I'm making myself a new office upstairs in Jonathan's old room. It's going to be a good year.

~

October 10, 1984
NEW YORK CITY

I've been thinking about my time in Germany again, unencumbered by artificial shades of terror and self-concern. I don't want my involvement with health matters to obscure the revelation of differences I encountered. The Afro-European women. What I learned about the differences when one teaches about feeling and poetry in a language that is not the original language of the people learning, even when they speak that language fluently. (Of course, all poets learn about feeling as children in our native tongue, and the psycho-social strictures and emotional biases of that language pass over into how we think about feeling for the rest of our lives.) I will never forget the emotional impact of Raja's poetry, and how what she is doing with the German language is so close to what Black poets here are doing with English. It was another example of how our African-ness impacts upon the world's consciousness in intersecting ways.

As an African-American woman, I feel the tragedy of being an oppressed hyphenated person in America, of having no land to be our primary teacher. And this distorts us in so many ways. Yet there is a vital part that we play as Black people in the liberation consciousness of every freedom-seeking people upon this globe, no matter what they say they think about us as Black Americans. And whatever our differences are that make for difficulty in communication between us and other oppressed peoples, as Afro-Americans we must recognize the promise we represent for some new social synthesis that the world has not yet experienced. I think of the Afro-Dutch, Afro-German, Afro-French women I met this spring in Europe, and how they are beginning to recognize each other and come together openly in terms of their identities, and I see that they are also beginning to cut a distinct shape across the cultural face of every country where they are at home.

I am thinking about issues of color as color, Black as a chromatic fact, gradations and all. There is the reality of defining Black as a geographical fact of culture and heritage emanating from the continent of Africa—Black meaning Africans and other members of a Diaspora, with or without color.

Then there is a quite different reality of defining Black as a political position, acknowledging that color is the bottom line the world over, no matter how many other issues exist alongside it. Within this definition, Black becomes a codeword, a rallying identity for all oppressed people of Color. And this position reflects the empowerment and the world-wide militant legacy of our Black Revolution of the 1960s, the effects of which are sometimes more obvious in other countries than in our own.

I see certain pitfalls in defining Black as a political position. It takes the cultural identity of a widespread but definite group and makes it a generic identity for many culturally diverse peoples, all on the basis of a shared oppression. This runs the risk of providing a convenient blanket of apparent similarity under which our actual and unaccepted differences can be distorted or misused. This blanket would diminish our chances of forming genuine working coalitions built upon the recognition and creative use of acknowledged difference, rather than upon the shaky foundations of a false sense of similarity. When a Javanese Dutch woman says she is Black, she also knows she goes home to another cultural reality that is particular to her people and precious to her—it is Asian, and Javanese. When an African-American woman says she is Black, she is speaking of her cultural reality, no matter how modified it may be by time, place, or circumstances of removal. Yet even the Maori women of New Zealand and the Aboriginal women of Australia call themselves Black.

There must be a way for us to deal with this, if only on the level of language. For example, those of us for whom Black is our cultural reality, relinquishing the word in favor of some other designation of the African Diaspora, perhaps simply *African*.

The first half of 1985 spins past: a trip to Cuba with a group of Black women writers, a reading tour through the Midwest, the great workspace I created from my son's old room, the beginning of a new collection of poems, my daughter's graduation from college. My general health seemed stable, if somewhat delicate. I removed the question of cancer from my consciousness beyond my regular Iscador treatments, my meager diet, and my lessened energies. In August and September I spent six weeks traveling and giving poetry readings in Australia and New Zealand, a guest of women's groups at various community organizations and universities. It was an exciting and exhausting time, one where thoughts about cancer were constant but never central.

~

May 28, 1985
CAMBRIDGE, MASSACHUSETTS

My daughter Beth's graduation from Harvard this weekend was a rite of passage for both of us. This institution takes itself very seriously, and there was enormous pomp and circumstance for three days. I couldn't help but think of all the racist, sexist ways they've tried through the last four years to diminish and destroy the essence of all the young Black women enrolled here. But it was a very important moment for Beth, a triumph that she'd survived Harvard, that she'd made it out, intact, and in a self she can continue living with. Of course, the point of so much of what goes on at places like Harvard—supposed to be about learning—is actually geared to either destroying these young people, or altering their substance into effigies that will be pliant, acceptable, and non-problematic to the system. So I was proud of Beth standing there in the manicured garden of Adams House, wearing her broad white Disinvestment banner across her black commencement gown, but I was also very scared for her. Out there can be even more difficult, although now she knows at least that she can and did survive Harvard. And with her own style unimpaired.

I embarrassed myself because I kept trying to find secret places to cry in, but it was still a very emotionally fulfilling occasion. I feel she's on her way now in a specific sense that must leave me behind, and that is both sad and very reassuring to me. I am convinced that Beth has the stuff—the emotional and psychic wherewithal to do whatever she needs to do for her living, and I have given her the best I have to offer. I remember writing "What My Child Learns of the Sea" when she was three months old, and it's both terrifying and wonderful to see it all coming true. I bless the goddess that I am still here to see it.

I tremble for her, for them all, because of the world we are giving them and all the work still to be done, and the gnawing question of will there be enough time? But I celebrate her, too, another one of those fine, strong, young Black women moving out to war, outrageous and resilient, plucky and beautiful.

I'm proud of her, and I'm proud of having seen her this far. It's a relief for me to know that whatever happens with my health now, and no matter how short my life may be, she is essentially on her way in the world, and next year Jonathan will be stepping out with his fine self, too. I look at them and they make my heart sing. Frances and I have done good work.

~

August 10, 1985
MELBOURNE, AUSTRALIA

A group of white Australian women writers invited me to give the keynote address on "The Language of Difference" at a Women's Writing Conference held in Melbourne as part of the 150-year celebration of the founding of the State of Victoria. These are my remarks:

> I am here upon your invitation, a Black African-American woman speaking of the language of difference. We come together in this place on the 150th Anniversary of the state of Victoria, an Australian State built upon racism, destruction, and a borrowed sameness. We were never meant to speak together at all. I have struggled for many weeks to find your part in me, to see what we could share that would have meaning for us all. When language becomes most similar, it becomes most dangerous, for then differences may pass unremarked. As women of good faith we can only become familiar with the language of difference within a determined commitment to its use within our lives, without romanticism and without guilt. Because we share a common language which is not of our own making

and which does not reflect our deeper knowledge as women, our words frequently sound the same. But it is an error to believe that we mean the same experience, the same commitment, the same future, unless we agree to examine the history and particular passions that lie beneath each other's words.

When I say I am Black, I mean I am of African descent. When I say I am a woman of Color, I mean I recognize common cause with American Indian, Chicana, Latina, and Asian-American sisters of North America. I also mean I share common cause with women of Eritrea who spend most of each day searching for enough water for their children, as well as with Black South African women who bury 50 percent of their children before they reach the age of five. And I also share cause with my Black sisters of Australia, the Aboriginal women of this land who were raped of their history and their children and their culture by a genocidal conquest in whose recognition we are gathered here today.

I have reached down deep inside of me to find what it was we could share, and it has been very difficult, because I find my tongue weighted down by the blood of my Aboriginal sisters that has been shed upon this earth. For the true language of difference is yet to be spoken in this place. Here that language must be spoken by my Aboriginal sisters, the daughters of those indigenous peoples of Australia with whom each one of you shares a destiny, but whose voices and language most of you here have never heard.

One hundred and fifty years ago, when the State of Victoria was declared a reality for European settlers, there were still 15,000 Black Aboriginal people living on this land that is now called Victoria. Where we sit now today, Wurundjeri women once dreamed and laughed and sang. They nurtured this earth, gum tree and wattle, and they were nurtured by it. I do not see their daughters sitting here among you today. Where are these women?

Their mothers' blood cries out to me. Their daughters come to my dreams nightly in the Windsor Hotel across the street from your Parliament. And their voices are haunting and brave and sad. Do you hear them? Listen very carefully, with your hearts open. They are speaking. Out of their mouths come what you have said you most want to hear.

Their history is my history. While white immigrant settlers in Australia were feeding Wurundjeri women and children bread made from arsenic and flour, white immigrant settlers in North America were selling seven-year-old African girls for $35 a head. And these same white immigrant settlers were giving blankets lethal with smallpox germs to the indigenous peoples of North America, the American Indians.

Each of you has come here today to touch some piece of your own power, for a purpose. I urge you to approach that work with a particular focus and urgency, for a terrible amount of Wurundjeri women's blood has already been shed in order for you to sit and write here.

I do not say these things to instigate an orgy of guilt, but rather to encourage an examination of what the excavation and use of the true language of difference can mean within your living. You and I can talk about the language of difference, but that will always remain essentially a safe discussion, because this is not my place. I will move on. But it is the language of the Black Aboriginal women of this country that you must learn to hear and to feel. And as your writing and your lives intersect within that language, you will come to decide what mistress your art must serve.

~

October 24, 1985
EAST LANSING, MICHIGAN

Tomorrow is the second anniversary of the invasion of Grenada. The smallest nation in the western hemisphere occupied by the largest. I spoke about it to a group of Black women here tonight. It's depressing to see how few of us remember, how few of us still seem to care.

The conference on "The Black Woman Writer and the Diaspora" being held here is problematic in some ways, particularly in the unclear position of Ellen Kuzwayo, who had come all the way from South Africa to give the keynote address and arrived here to find the schedule shifted. But it was so good to see Ellen again. I'm sorry to hear her sister in Botswana has had another mastectomy.

It's been very exciting to sit down with African and Caribbean women writers whom I've always wanted to meet. Octavia Butler is here also, and Andrea Canaan from New Orleans. I haven't seen her in over a year, and the look in her eyes when she saw me made me really angry, but it also made me realize how much weight I've lost in the past year and how bad my color's been since I came home from Australia. I've got to go see Dr. C. for a checkup when I get home.

~

October 25, 1985
EAST LANSING

I gave a brief talk tonight on "Sisterhood and Survival," what it means to me. And first off I identified myself as a Black Feminist Lesbian poet, although it felt unsafe, which is probably why I had to do it. I explained that I identified myself as such because if there was one other Black Feminist Lesbian poet in isolation somewhere within the reach of my voice, I wanted her to know she was not alone. I think a lot about Angelina Weld Grimké, a Black Lesbian poet of the Harlem Renaissance who is never identified as such, when she is mentioned at all, although the work of Gloria Hull and Erlene Stetson recently has focused renewed attention upon her. But I never even knew her name when I was going to school, and later, she was the briefest of mentions in a list of "other" Harlem Renaissance writers.

I often think of Angelina Weld Grimké dying alone in an apartment in New York City in 1958 while I was a young Black Lesbian struggling in isolation at Hunter College, and I think of what it could have meant in terms of sisterhood and survival for each one of us to have known of the other's existence: for me to have had her words and her wisdom, and for her to have known I needed them! It is so crucial for each one of us to know she is not alone. I've been traveling a lot in the last two years since my children are grown, and I've been learning what an enormous amount I don't know as a Black

American woman. And wherever I go, it's been so heartening to see women of Color reclaiming our lands, our heritages, our cultures, our selves—usually in the face of enormous odds.

For me as an African-American woman writer, sisterhood and survival means it's not enough to say I believe in peace when my sister's children are dying in the streets of Soweto and New Caledonia in the South Pacific. Closer to home, what are we as Black women saying to our sons and our nephews and our students as they are, even now, being herded into the military by unemployment and despair, someday to become meat in the battles to occupy the lands of other people of Color?

How can we ever, ever forget the faces of those young Black American soldiers, their gleaming bayonets drawn, staking out a wooden shack in the hills of Grenada? What is our real work as Black women writers of the Diaspora? Our responsibilities to other Black women and their children across this globe we share, struggling for our joint future? And what if our sons are someday ordered into Namibia, or Southwest Africa, or Zimbabwe, or Angola?

Where does our power lie and how do we school ourselves to use it in the service of what we believe?

Sitting with Black women from all over the earth has made me think a great deal about what it means to be indigenous, and what my relationship as a Black woman in North America is to the land-rights struggles of the indigenous peoples of this land, to Native American Indian women, and how we can translate that consciousness into a new level of working together. In other words, how can we use each other's differences in our common battles for a livable future?

All of our children are prey. How do we raise them not to prey upon themselves and each other? And this is why we cannot be silent, because our silences will come to testify against us out of the mouths of our children.

~

November 21, 1985
NEW YORK CITY

It feels like the axe is falling. There it is on the new CAT scan—another mass growing in my liver, and the first one is spreading. I've found an anthroposophic doctor in Spring Valley who suggests I go to the Lukas Klinik, a hospital in Switzerland where they are conducting the primary research on Iscador, as well as diagnosing and treating cancers.

I've known something is wrong from the returning pains and the dimming energies of my body. My classes have been difficult, and most days I feel like I'm going on sheer will power alone which can be very freeing and seductive but also very dangerous. Limited. I'm running down. But I'd do exactly what I'm doing anyway, cancer or no cancer.

A. will lend us the money to go to Switzerland, and Frances will come with me. I think they will be able to find out what is really wrong with me at the Lukas Klinik, and if they say these growths in my liver are malignant, then I will accept that I have cancer of the liver. At least there they will be able to adjust my Iscador dosage upward to the maximum effect, because that is the way I have decided to go and I'm not going to change now. Obviously, I still don't accept these tumors in my liver as cancer, although I know that could just be denial on my part, which is certainly one mechanism for coping with cancer. I have to consider denial as a possibility in all of my planning, but I also feel that there is absolutely nothing they can do for me at Sloane Kettering except cut me open and then sew me back up with their condemnations inside me.

~

December 7, 1985
NEW YORK CITY

My stomach x-rays are clear, and the problems in my GI series are all circumstantial. Now that the doctors here have decided I have liver cancer, they insist on reading all their findings as if that were a *fait accompli.* They refuse to look for any other reason for the irregularities in the x-rays, and they're treating my resistance to their diagnosis as a personal affront. But it's my body and my life and the goddess knows I'm paying enough for all this, I ought to have a say.

The flame is very dim these days. It's all I can do to teach my classes at Hunter and crawl home. Frances and I will leave for Switzerland as soon as school is over next week. The Women's Poetry Center will be dedicated at Hunter the night before I leave. No matter how sick I feel, I'm still afire with a need to do something for my living. How will I be allowed to live my own life, the rest of my life?

~

December 9, 1985
NEW YORK CITY

A better question is—how do I want to live the rest of my life and what am I going to do to insure that I get to do it exactly or as close as possible to how I want that living to be?

I want to live the rest of my life, however long or short, with as much sweetness as I can decently manage, loving all the people I love, and doing as much as I can of the work I still have to do. I am going to write fire until it comes out my ears, my eyes, my noseholes—everywhere. Until it's every breath I breathe. I'm going to go out like a fucking meteor!

~

December 13, 1985
NEW YORK CITY

There are some occasions in life too special to dissect, not only because they are everything they are supposed to be, but because they are also a sum of unexpected fantasies and deep satisfactions all come together at one point in time. Tonight the students of the Hunter College Women's Poetry Center Club and the *Returning Woman Newsletter* dedicated the Audre Lorde Women's Poetry Center. Walking into that hall, even thirty minutes late, was the beginning of exactly that kind of evening, and nothing I nor anyone else will ever do can lessen its meaning for me. Whatever happens to me, there has been a coming together in time and space of some of my best efforts, hopes, and desires. There is a tangible possibility to be built upon and strong young women committed to doing it. I wish them the power of their vision for what this Center can be in their lives and in the life of a community of women's culture in this city, the vision of a living women's poetry as a force for social change. This evening brought together four of my deepest and longest-lasting interests—poetry, beautiful women, revolution, and me!

No matter what I find out in Switzerland, no matter what's going on in my body, this is my work. The recognition of it, the sweet strength and love in the faces tonight make me know how much what I do has meant to these women who are arming themselves to walk in places I've only dreamed of, and in their own step and as their own mistresses.

I listened tonight to these young poets, particularly the women of Color, reading their work, and it was wonderful for me to know that the real power of my words is not the pieces of me that reside within those words, but the life-force—the energy and aspirations and desires at the complex core of each one of these women—which has been aroused to use and to answer my words. Gloria, Johnnetta, and I—three of the Founding Mothers of the Sisterhood in Support of Sisters in South Africa—within that precious space where we sit down together in my intricate life. The young poets shining like goldfire in the sun, their many-colored faces awash with pride and determination and love. Beth and Yolanda, daughter and old friend, my words coming out of their mouths illuminated exactly by who they are themselves, so different from each other and from me. The revelation of hearing my work translated through the beings of these women I love so dearly. Frances, smiling like a sunflower and really there; my sister Helen looking pleased and a part of it all; and Mabel Hampton, tough and snappy and hanging in, all eighty-three years of her! Charlotte's generous perfume, and I remember the sureness in her voice once, saying, "Well, we did what we had to do, and I think we changed the world!" Alexis and her twinkling eyes, Clare's warm graciousness. And Blanchie, resplendent and cheeky in her tuxedo, orchestrating it all with her particular special flair, Mistress of Ceremonies to quite a party!

December 15, 1985
ARLESHEIM, SWITZERLAND

So here I am at the Lukas Klinik while my body decides if it will live or die. I'm going to fight like hell to make it live, and this looks like the most promising possibility. At least it's something different from narcotics and other terminal aids, which is all Dr. C. had to offer me in New York City in lieu of surgery when I told her how badly I hurt in my middle. "Almost everything I eat now makes me sick," I told her. "Yes, I know," she said sorrowfully, writing me a prescription for codeine and looking at me as if there was nothing left she could do for me besides commiserate. Even though I like her very much, I wanted to punch her in her mouth.

I have found something interesting in a book here on active meditation as a form of self-control. There are six steps:

1. Control of Thought

    Think of a small object (i.e., a paper clip) for five minutes, exclusively. Practice for a month.

2. Control of Action

    Perform a small act every day at the same time. Practice, and be patient.

3. Control of Feeling (equanimity)

    Become aware of feelings and introduce equanimity into experiencing them—i.e., be afraid, not panic-stricken. (They're big on this one around here.)

4. Positivity (tolerance)

    Refrain from critical downgrading thoughts that sap energy from good work.

73

5. Openness (receptivity)
   Perceive even what is unpleasant in an unfettered, non-prejudiced way.
6. Harmony (perseverance)
   Work toward balancing the other five.

As a living creature I am part of two kinds of forces—growth and decay, sprouting and withering, living and dying, and at any given moment of our lives, each one of us is actively located somewhere along a continuum between these two forces.

~

December 16, 1985
ARLESHEIM

I brought some of my books with me, and reading *The Cancer Journals* in this place is like excavating words out of the earth, like turning up a crystal that has been buried at the bottom of a mine for a thousand years, waiting. Even *Our Dead Behind Us*—now that it has gone to the printer—seems prophetic. Like always, it feels like I plant what I will need to harvest, without consciousness.

This is why the work is so important. Its power doesn't lie in the me that lives in the words so much as in the heart's blood pumping behind the eye that is reading, the muscle behind the desire that is sparked by the word—hope as a living state that propels us, open-eyed and fearful, into all the battles of our lives. And some of those battles we do not win.

But some of them we do.

December 17, 1985
ARLESHEIM

When I read in Basel last June, I never imagined I would be here again, four miles away, in a hospital. I remember the women in the bookstore that night, and their questions about survival rates that I could not answer then. And certainly not now.

Even in the bleak Swiss winter, the grounds of the Lukas Klinik are very beautiful. Much care has been given by the builders to the different shades of winter scenery, so there is a play of light and dark that hits the eye from the room's windows as well as from the beds. My private room is good-sized, spacious by American hospital standards. It is one of the few single rooms with a private bath, and they are usually for very sick or very rich people. I think the administration was not sure which category I fit into when I called fromNew York.

Even when it is not sunny, the room is light because everything in it is light. Not white, except for the bedsheets, but very light. Even the furniture is solid hand-hewn blond wood, made in one of the sheltered workshops run in conjunction with an anthroposophic school for developmentally handicapped people. The Rudolf Steiner schools have had great success in the area of Special Education.

There is a deep serenity here, relaxing and sometimes uncomfortable. The adjustable hospital bed is covered with a voluptuous down comforter under which a hot-water bottle had been slipped the first night I arrived. And six red rosebuds in a cut-glass vase. On the other side of the bedside table is an easy chair, and then a wide window and a glass door opening onto terraces that run the length of each of the tiered three stories of the building. The tiers provide plenty of sunlight on each floor. There are opaque dividers for privacy between the doors leading onto the terrace, and then a common strollway open to the sky.

Beneath the terraces is a carefully tended European garden, sculptured stone steps cut into one side winding back and forth through the low bushes and plantings throughout the grounds. In the grassy clearing in front of the terraces stands a red granite statue of a robed person with what I have come to think of as the Steiner look, blunt and massive, one arm upraised in the eurhythmic position for the vowel *i* which is considered in all languages to be the sound representing the affirmation of self in living. On a slight knoll, the statue is silhouetted against the green trees or the leaden sky.

At the foot of the statue and to one side is a large oval whirlpool fountain of red granite also, its perennial gurgle of softly flowing water a soothing counterpoint whenever the terrace door is opened, or when walking through the grounds.

A quite lovely pastel painting of a sunrise hangs on one wall of the room, executed according to the Rudolf Steiner theory of color and healing. It is the only wall decoration in the room, whose walls are painted a sunny yellow and peach.

Most of the patients are middle-aged Swiss and Germans, with two French women and myself. We all wear our own clothes. There is a large sitting room that contains a library, and a chapel, of course, and appropriate Steiner reading materials always available.

Everyone who works with patients gives off a similar affect: it is calm, kind, and helpful, but also completely dogmatic. Staff, patients, and visitors eat lunch and dinner together in a spacious, well-draped but sunny dining room with real linens and individualized embroidered napkins. We are seated at tables holding six to ten diners, amid signs of the zodiac and planets sculpted from various kinds of European bedrock, also done in the Steiner artistic tradition of massive, solid lines.

Meals are a real chore for me, since it is difficult for me to eat anyway and I loathe eating around strangers. The feeling in the dining room is genteel, cultivated, and totally formal.

I take a one-and-a-half-hour class daily in Curative Eurhythmy with a tiny East Indian woman named Dilnawaz who was raised in Rudolf Steiner schools in India, trained in Germany, and speaks fluent English and German as well as her native tongue.

Eurhythmy is a combination of sustained rhythmical body movements and controlled breathing, based upon vowel and consonant sounds. As I learn and practice the stylized movements, they remind me of Tai Chi and feel like a complement to the Simonton visualization work I've been doing for a while. My body feels relaxed and good after eurhythmy, and my mind, too.

There is a part of me that wants to dismiss everything here other than Iscador as irrelevant or at least not useful to me, even before I try it, but I think that is very narrow and counterproductive and I don't want to do it. At least not without first giving myself fully to it, because that is why I came all this way and what do I have to lose at this point? Dilnawaz stresses that the treatment of any disease, and of cancer in particular, must be all of a piece, body and mind, and I am ready to try anything so long as they don't come at me with a knife.

Dilnawaz is the most human, the most friendly, and the most real person I've met here, as well as the most spiritual. She is also the most lonely. She is very friendly and helpful toward everyone, and people respond to her with considerable respect, but there is still an air of isolation about her that says to me she is not quite a part. She lives alone in Arlesheim town, and her sister is coming from Germany to spend Christmas with her.

I wonder how she feels as a woman of Color among all these white ethnocentric Swiss. She is very cautious about what she says, but she does talk of how reluctant most Northern Europeans are to give themselves to eurhythmy. I find her a touch of emotional color within a scene of extraordinary blandness.

Dilnawaz seems to be relieved to see me, too. I think she knows I have a deep respect for the spiritual aspect of our lives and its power over us. That is something most of the rationalists here do not have, despite their adherence to Steiner's anthroposophy. It seems they can only deal with spirituality if it comes with rigid rules imposed from the outside, i.e. Steiner, with his insistence upon the basic rule of a Christian god. It is limiting.

I take a class in painting and color theory according to Steiner. Afterward, an oil dispersion bath which alternates with a massage (also according to Steiner), then lunch, a hot yarrow liver poultice and a two-hour rest period. Then I am free until dinner, unless there are medical consultations or tests. This is when Frances and I get to see each other privately for a while.

There are about fifty patients here right now, and about fifteen doctors, as well as some visiting doctors and medical trainees from different countries. The calm directness with which everyone seems to deal with the idea and reality of disease is quite unlike anything I've experienced in hospitals in the U.S., given that all the patients here either have cancer or are suspected of having cancer. At its best, the effect of this directness is very calming and reassuring, very centering. At its worst, it feels like

Mann's *Magic Mountain*. Because at the same time, nobody believes in talking about feelings, even the strong expression of which is considered to be harmful, or at least too stressful to be beneficial.

In the private room next door to me, there is a pretty young Swiss woman of no more than twenty, with a gold wedding band on and very expensive clothes and too much make-up. She appears terribly depressed all the time. Evidently she goes to church in town every morning, because I see her passing through the grounds early each day wearing a church cap. Her family seems very rich or very influential. They came to visit yesterday, and I saw them in the dining room—mother, father, and a young man who was either brother or husband. They sure looked rich, and everyone here bowed and scraped to them. (The social hierarchy is quite strongly observed.) It seems to me that anyone that young who has cancer must be filled with rage and should at least be able to talk about her feelings with someone. But that's not considered necessary or beneficial here.

There is an elderly woman schoolteacher from Hamburg who wears a beautifully carved rhodonite necklace to lunch every day. We have had an interesting conversation about rocks and minerals, which are considered to be very important and powerful in anthroposophy. She speaks English quite well and tries to be friendly. She has been an anthroposoph for many years, she says, and this is her second stay at the Klinik.

The most frequent question from English-speaking patients and medical trainees, couched in different ways, is: How does an American—and a Black one at that, although the latter is only inferred because everyone here is much too well-bred and polite to ever let on they notice, although sister Maria did tell me yesterday that her brother is a missionary in South Africa so she understands why I like to eat raw vegetables—how does an American come to be at the Lukas Klinik in Switzerland? Americans are known for being quite provincial.

One of the cardinal rules here is that we do not talk about our illness at mealtimes or at any social gathering, so everyone is very polite and small-talky and banal, because of course we are all pre-occupied with our bodies and the processes going on within them or else we wouldn't be here. I don't know what makes the anthro-posophs think this sort of false socializing is not more stressful than expressing real feelings, but I find it terribly wearing. Mercifully, I can usually retreat behind the language barrier.

~

December 19, 1985
ARLESHEIM

I sit lie paint walk dance weep in a Swiss hospital trying to find out what my body wants to do, waiting for doctors to come talk with me. Last night my stomach and liver cried all night. "So this is the way of dying," I thought, my body feeling almost transparent. In the sun-light now I think someone was dying next door, and I felt the sadness through the walls coupled with my own. When the sun came up I felt a lot better, until I saw the bed stripped down in the hallway, and the next-door buzzer silent at last.

The village of Arlesheim is very lovely and picturesque. Frances and I go for long walks in the park holding hands in our coat pockets, giving each other courage, and wondering about the future. I have written no letters, no poems, no journals except these notes, trying to make sense out of it all.

I am often in pain and I fear that it will get worse. I need to sharpen every possible weapon against it, but even more so against the fear, or the fear of fear, which is what is so debilitating. And I want to learn how to do that while there is still time for learning in some state before desperation. Desperation. Reckless through despair.

There is no more time left to decide upon strange afflictions.

~

December 20, 1985
ARLESHEIM

A men's choir from the village sang Christmas carols tonight in the hospital stairwells, their voices echoing through the halls, sweet and poignant, and I cried for Christmases I have had that are past. But I simply cannot allow myself to believe that there will never be any more of them, so there surely must be. How different this season is from any holiday season I could possibly have foreseen. Dear Goddess! How many more?

Frances' being here makes it complete in an essential way no matter what, and at least we can wander about the village in the afternoons together looking at the shops, or walk the hills enjoying the countryside and the manicured little winter gardens. I stretch to be able to appreciate the loveliness in its own—European—right, before it is gone, too, and I no longer have a chance to explore it for whatever it can mean for me.

Audre Lorde

December 21, 1985
ARLESHEIM

I sleep well here when I sleep. Yesterday was another horrendous communal dinner. Difficult as it is for me to get anything down, I find the genteel smugness, the sameness, infuriating. It's better now that Frances has started taking her meals here with me. At least we can talk to each other.

I had to do battle between the soup and the salad with an Australian pig who proved that racism is as alive and well in Arlesheim as it was on that wretched bus in Melbourne when that drunken Aussie accosted me thinking I was *Koori* (Aborigine).

The choir really got to me tonight, mellow and measured and very civilized, so long as you accept their terms of living and their way of life and values. The sweet voices, the smell of pine and the lovely candle arrangements with red and green holly in every hallway, the Christmas decorations in all the corridors, the determined cheerfulness. Nurses go around and open every door a bit so that everyone can hear the music. Soft lights shining in the twilight windows. Very lovely. Just don't be different. Don't even think about being different. It's bad for you.

Today is the day the sun returns. Sweet Solstice. Mother, arm me for whatever is ahead of me. Let me at the very least be equal to it, if not totally in charge of changing it. Last night Gloria called. As she said, take whatever you can use there and let the rest go.

Another choir is singing now in the halls. If I had the strength, I would get up from this bed and run out into the starlit freezing night and keep running until I collapsed into a heap of huffs and

82

puffs of effort and strained muscles. But I can't quite manage that, and Frances has gone back to her hotel, and my heart aches from strangeness. The sound of these voices singing familiar melodies in a foreign tongue only reminds me of the distance between me and my familiar places.

Yet this is the only place I know right now that offers me any hope, and that will treat me and my liver seriously.

~

December 22, 1985
ARLESHEIM

I have brought some of my stones and macramé threads with me. I've laid out the stones on my windowsill, and they are beautiful in the light. I'm going to make a new healing necklace for myself from them while I'm here, and I'm going to make the heart-piece from carnelian, which is a specific against melancholy. And that's my answer to Sister Marie's cautioning me against the dangers of an excess of joy!

It's the nights after Frances goes back to the hotel that are the hardest. I spend my day racing around between those dreadful public meals and the eurhythmics and painting and baths and tests and running over to Frances' hotel for a quick cuddle then back here for a liver compress or to take my temperature or something else equally vital in this half-seen scheme of things that feels like a pact I've made with myself to do as they believe is best for a stated period of time—three weeks. In other words, to give the Lukas Klinik my best shot because it is the only thing I have going for me right now, and tomorrow the results from all my liver tests and other diagnostic analyses will be back. I haven't really thought about what they will be because I just can't spend any more energy in being scared.

What I have to fight the hardest against here is feeling that it is just not worth it—too much fight for too little return, and I hurt all the damn time. Something is going on inside me, and it's interfering with my life. There is a persistent and pernicious despair hovering over me constantly that feels physiological, even when my basic mood is quite happy. I don't understand it, but I do not want to slip or fall into any kind of resignation. I am not going to go gently into anybody's damn good night!

~

December 23, 1985, 10:30 a.m.
ARLESHEIM

I have cancer of the liver.

Dr. Lorenz just came in and told me. The crystallization test and the liver sonogram are all positive. The two masses in my liver are malignant. He says I should begin an increased Iscador program and antihormone therapy right away, if I decide that is the way I want to go. Well. The last possibility of doubt based on belief is gone. I said I'd come to Lukas because I trusted the anthroposophic doctors, and if they said it was malignant then I would accept their diagnosis. So here it is, and all the yelling and head-banging isn't going to change it. I guess it helps to finally know. I wish Frances were here.

I cannot afford to waste any more time in doubting, or in fury. The question is what do I do now? Listen to my body, of course, but the messages get dimmer and dimmer. In two weeks I go back home. Iscador or chemotherapy or both?

How did I ever come to be in this place? What can I use it for?

~

December 24, 1985
ARLESHEIM

I feel trapped on a lonely star. Someone else is very sick next door, and the vibes are almost too painful to bear. But I must stop saying that now so glibly. Someday something will, in fact, be too painful to bear and then I will have to act. Does one simply get tired of living? I can't imagine right now what that would be like, but that is because I feel filled with a fury to live—because I believe life can be good even when it is painful—a fury that my energies just don't match my desires anymore.

~

December 25, 1985
ARLESHEIM

Good morning, Christmas. A Swiss bubble is keeping me from talking to my children and the women I love. The front desk won't put my calls through. Nobody here wants to pierce this fragile, delicate bubble that is the best of all possible worlds, they believe. So frighteningly insular. Don't they know good things get better by opening them up to others, giving and taking and changing? Most

85

people here seem to feel that rigidity is a bona fide pathway to peace, and every fibre of me rebels against that.

~

December 26, 1985
ARLESHEIM

Adrienne and Michelle and Gloria just called from California. I feel so physically cut off from the people I love. I need them, the sharing of grief and energy.

I am avoiding plunging directly into the nightmare of liver cancer as a fact of my life by edging into it like an icy bath. I am trying to edge my friends into it, too, without having to deal with more of their fury and grief than I can handle. There is some we share, and that mutual support makes us closer and more resolved. But there is some that they will have to deal with on their own, just as there is some fury and grief that I can only meet in a private place. Frances has been so true and staunch here. It is more difficult for her sometimes because she does not have the fount of desperate determination that survival is generating inside me.

There is so much to keep track of. I think it's crucial that I not only suffer this but record, in the fullness and the lean, some of the raw as well as digested qualities of now.

Last night there was a Christmas full moon, and it felt like a hopeful sign. I stood out in the road in front of the hospital under the full moon on Christmas night and thought about all of my beloved people, the women I love, my children, my family, all the dear faces before my eyes. The moon was so clear and bright, I could feel her upon my skin through Helen's fur coat.

After I had gone to bed she called me back to her twice. The first time I could not pierce through the veil of sleep, but I saw her light and heard her in my dreams. Then at 4:30 in the morning, her little fingers of light reached under the lined window curtains, and I got up as if bidden and went out onto the terrace to greet her. The night was very very still; she was low and bright and brilliantly clear. I stood on the terrace in my robe bathed in her strong quiet light. I raised my arms then and prayed for us all, prayed for the strength for all of us who must weather this time ahead with me. My mother moon had awakened me, calling me out into her brightness, and she shone down upon me as a sign, a blessing on that terrace with the soft gurgle of flowing water in my ears, a promise of answering strength to be whoever I need to be. I felt her in my heart, in my bones, in my thin blood, and I heard Margareta's voice again: "It's going to be a hard lonely road, but remember, help is on the way." That was her farewell Tarot reading for me, seventeen years ago.

~

December 27, 1985
ARLESHEIM

Last night I dreamed I was asleep here in my bed at the Klinik and there was a strange physical presence lying beside me on the left side. I couldn't see it because it was dark, but I felt this body start to touch me on my left thigh, and I knew that this meant great danger. "It must think I'm dead so it can have (claim) me," I thought, "but if I moan it will know I'm awake and alive and it'll leave me alone." So I began to moan softly, but the creature didn't stop. I could feel its cold fingers beginning to creep over my left hip, and I thought to

87

myself, "Oh, oh, nightmare time! I've got to scream louder. Maybe that noise will make it go away, because there is nobody else here to wake me up!" So I screamed and roared in my sleep, and finally after what seemed like a very long time, I woke myself up calling out, and of course there was nothing in my bed at all, but it still felt as if death had really been trying.

~

December 30, 1985
ARLESHEIM

Frances and I went to the Konditorei in town this afternoon to have a cup of tea and be together away from the hospital, when the elderly schoolteacher with the rhodonite necklace came in and wanted to sit down with us. It was so apparent how badly she wanted to talk that we couldn't say no, even though we never have enough time alone together.

It was actually quite sad. Dr. Lorenz had just told her that her breast cancer has spread to her bones, and she doesn't know what she is going to do. She has to make plans for her elderly mother for whom she now cares at home but will no longer be able to. There is no one she knows to whom she can turn for help because her sister died last year. I felt very sorry for her. Here it is, almost New Year's Eve, and there isn't even anyone she can talk to about her worries except two strange Americans in a teashop.

Then she went on to explain that she and her sister had had to live with foreign workers (she meant Italians) in the factory where they worked during World War II, and that the foreigners were very dirty, with lice and fleas, so she and her sister would sprinkle DDT in their hair and their beds every night so as not to catch diseases! And she is sure that is why the cancer has spread to her bones now. There was something so grotesque about this sad lonely old woman dying of bone cancer still holding on to her ethnic prejudices, even when she was realizing that they were going to cost her her life. The image of her as a young healthy aryan bigot was at war inside me with the pathetic old woman at our table, and I had to get out of there immediately.

~

December 31, 1985
ARLESHEIM

Old Year's Day, the last day of this troubled year. And yes, all the stories we tell are about healing in some form or the other.

In this place that makes such a point of togetherness and community, Frances and I sat through an ornate New Year's Eve dinner tonight surrounded by empty chairs on each side of us, an island unto ourselves in the festive hall. It's good that we have each other, but why should I have to suffer through this ostracism and pay for it as well? I guess because the point is not that I enjoy it but that I gain from it, and that's up to me. As Gloria said on the phone, "Take what you can use and let the rest GO!" They don't have to love me, just help me.

My Maori jade tiki is gone forever, either lost or stolen from my room. How much more do I have to lose before it is enough?

I cannot bear to think that this might be my last New Year's Eve. But it might be. What a bummer! But if that's true at least I have had others which were sweet and fall past comparing, and filled with enough love and promise to last forever and beyond me. Frances, Beth and Jonathan, Helen, Blanche and Clare, our loving circle. I hold now to what I know and have always known in my heart ever since I first knew what loving was—that when it truly exists it is the most potent and lasting force in life, even if certainly not the fastest. But without it nothing else is worth a damn.

After Frances went back to the hotel I washed my hair (wishing I had some white flowers to put in the water for a blessing), listened to Bob Marley, and went to bed.

> . . .*this is my message to you-u-u-u-u-u,*
> *every lil thing------is gon be allright-t-t-t. . .*

~

January 1, 1986
ARLESHEIM

Today Frances and I hiked to the top of a mountain to see the Dornach ruins, and the whole Rhine valley spread out beneath us. It felt so good to be moving my body again. My mother always used to say that whatever you do on New Year's Day you will do all year round, and I'd certainly like to believe that's true.

It was very cold and sunny and bright, three miles up and back. The ruins rang with that historical echo and the presence of trials labored and past, although not as profoundly as the stones of El Morro in Cuba, and certainly not as desperately as the walls of Elmina Castle in Ghana, from whence so many Black women and children and men were sent to hell—slavery.

February 20, 1986
ANGUILLA, BRITISH WEST INDIES

I am here seeking sun on my bones. A dry little island with outland-
ishly beautiful beaches, and soft-voiced West Indian people living
their lives by the sea. Anguilla's primary source of income is from
import duties, second comes fishing. I go out at dawn to see the fish-
ermen put out from Crocus Bay, and when they return they sometimes give Gloria and me fish. An intricate network of ownership
and shares governs the dividing up of each catch.

Fossilized sand dollars wash out of the sand banks onto the
beaches of Anguilla and out of the claystone bluffs that grade down-
ward toward the beach. I spend hours wandering the beaches and
searching for them, or collecting shells that I rinse at the water's
green edge. I would never have known about this island except for
Gloria. Anguilla feels like a piece of home, a very healing, restful
place, but with the rich essences of life.

The sun and the sea here are helping me save my life. They are a
far softer cry from the East River, Spuyten Duyvil, and the Lower
New York Bay. But always, the sea speaks to me no matter where I
get to her. I suppose that is a legacy of my mother's, from when we
used to stand, all those years ago, staring out over the sooty pebbles
at the foot of 142nd Street and the Harlem River. Anguilla reminds
me of Carriacou, the tiny island off the coast of Grenada where my
mother was born.

When I am next to the sea, the wide spread of water laps over me
with an enduring peace and excitement that feels like finding some
precious rock in the earth, a sense of touching something that is

most essentially me in a place where my past and my future intersect along the present. The present, that line of stress and connection and performance, the intense crashing now. Yet only earth and sky last forever, and the ocean joins them.

I hear the waters' song, feel the tides within the fluids of my body, hear the sea echoing my mothers' voices of survival form Elmina to Grenville to Harlem. I hear them resounding inside me from swish to boom—from the dark of the moon to fullness.

~

April 2, 1986
ST. CROIX, VIRGIN ISLANDS

This is the year I spent spring beachcombing in St. Croix, awash with the trade winds and coconuts, sand and the sea. West Indian voices in the supermarket and Chase Bank, and the Caribbean flavors that have always meant home. Healing within a network of Black women who supplied everything from a steady stream of tender coconuts to spicy gossip to sunshine to fresh parrot fish to advice on how to cool out from academic burnout to a place where I can remember how the earth feels at 6:30 in the morning under a tropical crescent moon working in the still-cool garden—a loving context within which I fit and thrive.

I have been invited to take part in a conference on Caribbean women, "The Ties That Bind." At first I didn't think I'd have the energy to do it, but the whole experience has been a powerful and nourishing reminder of how good it feels to be doing my work where I'm convinced it matters the most, among the women—my sisters—who I most want to reach. It feels like I'm talking to Helen, my sister, and Carmen, my cousin, with all the attendant frustrations and joys rolled up together. It's always like this when you're trying to get people you love mightily to hear and use the ways in which you all are totally different, knowing they are the most difficult to reach. But it is the ways in which you are the same that make it possible to communicate at all.

The conference was organized by Gloria and the other three Sojourner Sisters, and it's an incredible accomplishment for four Black women with full-time jobs elsewhere to have pulled together such an ambitious enterprise. They orchestrated the entire event, bringing together presenters from ten different countries, feeding and housing us royally, as well as organizing four days of historical, cultural, and political presentations and workshops that were enjoyable and provocative for the more than 200 women who attended.

Johnetta Cole's moving presentation of the Cuban revolution and its meaning in the lives of Caribbean women; Merle Hodges' incisive analysis of the sexism in calypsos; Dessima Williams, former Ambassador from Grenada to the Organization of American States, proud and beautiful, recalling Maurice Bishop and Grenadian liberation with tears in her eyes.

In addition to being a tremendous high, these days are such a thrilling example to me of the real power of a small group of Black women of the Diaspora in action. Four community women, meeting after work for almost a year, dreamed, planned, financed, and executed this conference without institutional assistance. It has been an outstanding success, so much information and affirmation for those of us who participated as well as for those of us who attended.

It was a very centering experience for me, an ideal place for me to step out again, and I was so proud to be a part of it, and to speak and read my work as a Caribbean woman.

April 5, 1986
ST. CROIX

Yesterday was the eighteenth anniversary of Martin Luther King's murder. Carnegie Hall, Duke Ellington, the Tougaloo Choir. Their young Black voices tear in my blood to this day. *What the world needs now is love. . . .* There was still a space left for hope then, but the shore was fading fast. I wonder where all those kids from Tougaloo are now who stood so brave and tearful and together in their aloneness. I wonder how each of their lives is being influenced/formed/informed by the emotions and events upon that stage of Carnegie Hall that night King died. I wonder if I will ever hear from any one of them again.

~

April 20, 1986
ST. CROIX

Blanchie's birthday. When Blanche had her mastectomy last year, it was the first time that I had to face, in a woman I loved, feelings and fears I had faced within my own self, but never dealt with externally. Now I had to speak to these feelings in some way that was meaningful and urgent in the name of my love. Somehow I had known for the past eight years that someday it would be this way, that personal salvation of whatever kind is never *just* personal.

I talked with Blanchie today over the phone about this feeling I have that I must rally everything I know, made alive and immediate with the fire of what is.

I have always been haunted by the fear of not being able to reach the women I am closest to, of not being able to make available to the women I love most dearly what I can make available to so many others. The women in my family, my closest friends. If what I know to be true cannot be of use to them, can it ever have been said to be true at all? On the other hand, that lays a terrible burden on all of us concerned, doesn't it?

It is a matter of learning languages, or of learning to use them with precision to do what needs to be done with them, and it is the Blanchie in myself to whom I need to speak with such urgency. It's one of the great things friends are for each other when you've been very close for a long time.

And of course cancer is political—look at how many of our comrades have died of it during the last ten years! As warriors, our job is to actively and consciously survive it for as long as possible, remembering that in order to win, the aggressor must conquer, but the resisters need only survive. Our battle is to define survival in ways that are acceptable and nourishing to us, meaning with substance and style. Substance. Our work. Style. True to our selves.

What would it be like to be living in a place where the pursuit of definition within this crucial part of our lives was not circumscribed and fractionalized by the economics of disease in America? Here the first consideration concerning cancer is not what does this mean in my living, but how much is this going to cost?

~

April 22, 1986
ST. CROIX

I got a letter from Ellen Kuzwayo this morning. Her sister in Botswana has died. I wish I were in Soweto to put my arms around her and rest her head on my shoulder. She sounds so strong and sanguine in her unshakable faith, yet so much alone. In the fabric of horrors that she and the other women live through daily in South Africa, this loss takes its place among so many others, at the same time particular and poignant.

~

May 8, 1986
NEW YORK CITY

Tomorrow belongs to those of us who conceive of it as belonging to everyone; who lend the best of ourselves to it, and with joy.

It takes all of my selves, working together, to integrate what I learn of women of Color around the world into my consciousness and work. It takes all of my selves working together to effectively focus attention and action against the holocaust progressing in South Africa and the South Bronx and Black schools across this nation, not to speak of the streets. Laying myself on the line. It takes all of my selves working together to fight this death inside me. Every one of these battles generates energies useful in the others.

I am on the cusp of change, and the curve is shifting fast.

In the bleakest days I am kept afloat, maintained, empowered, by the positive energies of so many women who carry the breath of my loving like firelight in their strong hair.

~

May 23, 1986
NEW YORK CITY

I spoke with Andrea in New Orleans this morning. She and Diana are helping to organize a Black Women's Book Fair. Despite its size, there is not one feminist bookstore in the whole city. She's very excited about the project, and it was a real charge talking to her about it. There are so many young Black women across this country stepping out wherever they may be and making themselves felt within their communities in very real ways. These women make the early silence and the doubts and the wear and tear of it all worth it. I feel like they are my inheritors, and sometimes I breathe a sigh of relief that they exist, that I don't have to do it all.

It's a two-way street, and even I don't always realize it. Like the little sister from AA who stood up at my poetry reading last week and talked about how much courage I'd given her, and I was quaking in my boots because when she began I'd thought she was about to lay a heavy cancer rap on me in public, and I just wasn't quite ready for that yet. I feel very humbled behind that little episode. I want to acknowledge all those intricate connections between us by which we sustain and empower each other.

⁓

June 20, 1986
BONNIEUX, FRANCE

How incredibly rich to be here in the south of France with the Zamani Soweto Sisters from South Africa. Gloria and I became acquainted with them through Ellen Kuzwayo and our fundraising work with the Sisterhood in Support of Sisters in South Africa. They are one of the groups we help support through contributions. I'm only sorry that Ellen couldn't be here also, but at least I had a chance to share time and space with her in London on June 16th, the anniversary of the Soweto Uprising.

I learn tremendous courage from these women, from their laughter and their tears, from their grace under constant adversity, from their joy in living which is one of their most potent weapons, from the deft power of their large, overworked bodies and their dancing, swollen feet. In this brief respite for us all made possible by Betty Wolpert's kindness, these women have taught me so much courage and perspective.

~

June 21, 1986
BONNIEUX

Sweet Solstice, and again the goddess smiles upon me. I am sitting in the stone-ringed yard of Les Quelles, a beautiful old reclaimed silk factory, now a villa. Gloria and the women of the Zamani Soweto Sisters surround me, all of us brilliant and subtle under the spreading flowers of a lime-tea tree. It looks and feels like what I've always imagined the women's compound in some African village to have been, once. Some of us drink tea, some are sewing, sweeping the dirt ground of the yard, hanging out clothes in the sunlight at the edge of the enclosure, washing, combing each other's hair. Acacia blossoms perfume the noon air as Vivian tells the stories behind the tears in her glowing amber eyes.

The young students who do not ask their parents' permission to run in the streets and die. The wealthy Black undertaker who lends his funeral hearses to the police to transport the bodies of the slain children.

The three little children who saw a heavy-armored Caspir barreling down the road in Dube and ran to hide behind the silk-cotton tree at the edge of the yard, too young to know that they could be seen as the tank rolled down the road. The blond policeman leaning out from the side of the tank to fire behind the tree at the little ones as they hid, reaching back over his shoulder to fire again as the vehicle rolled along, just to make sure the babies were all dead.

She tells of the mothers in her street who stay home from work risking deportation to the barrenness of an alien "homeland," trudging from police station to police station all over Soweto asking, "Are my children here? Please sirs, this is her picture this is his school name he is nine years of age are my children here?" Her son leaving detention dragging his heels forever, achilles tendons torn and festering from untreated police dog bites.

Ruth, majestic and proud as Mujaji, ancient rain queen of the Lovedu. "I write my thoughts down on little scraps of paper," she says, talking about where the ideas come from for her intricate quilts. "And sometimes I pull them all out and read them and then I say no, that's not it at all and I throw them right away. But other times I smooth them out and save them for the quilts. I would like to keep a whole book of these stories from my life, but then a quilt is like a book of many stories done up together, and many people can read it all at the same time."

Gentle, strong, beautiful—the women of Soweto imprint their faces and their courage upon me. They enhance this French air, a cloud of soap and cosmetics and the lightest hint of hair cream. The knowledge of struggle never distant. Womanliness pervades this space.

Thembi, called Alice, flames under her taut sweetness, walking a dangerously narrow path too close to the swamp where there are bright lights flashing like stars just below the murky surface in harmony with the voices of astonished frogs in the green night. She begs me to release her from the pain of not doing enough for our own, of not making our daughters into ourselves. She tells me to dream upon all of their stories and write them a poem.

Petal, whose eyes are often too quiet as she moves about, short, solid, and graceful. We discuss love, comparing tales, and her eyes flash, amused and aglow. Other times they are wary, filled with distrust and grieving. Petal, who bore seven children and only two live. Who was tortured for weeks by the South African police. Who was helped by the International Hospital for Torture Victims in Switzerland.

Sula, wry and generous, knows how to get any question answered with a gentle inescapable persistence. Sometimes she drinks a lot. Her first husband broke her heart, but she quickly married again. "The missionaries lied to us so much about our bodies," she said, indignantly, "telling us they were dirty and we had to cover them up, and look now who is running about in bikinis on the Riviera, or naked and topless! I had a friend. . . ," and she starts another story, like one most of these women tell, of a special woman friend who loved her past explaining.

Sweet-faced Emily tells of the militant young comrades in Soweto, their defiance of the old ways, carrying their determination for change into the streets. She demonstrates for us a spirited and high-stepping rendition of their rousing machine-gun dance.

She does not like to listen to the other women singing hymns. Emily, who loved her best friend so much she still cannot listen to the records they once enjoyed together, and it is five years already since her friend died.

Linda of the hypnotic eyes who was questioned once by the South African police every single day for an entire month. About Zamani Soweto Sisters and subversive activities, such as a tiny ANC flag stitched on the little dead boy's pocket in the corner of a funeral procession quilt. "The quilts tell stories from our own lives. We did not know it was forbidden to sew the truth, but we will caution the women never to stitch such a thing again. No, thank you, I do not wish to take a cup of tea with you." I can hear her grave dignity speaking. She finishes the tale with a satisfied laugh.

Linda has a nineteen-year-old daughter. The women joke and offer us their daughters to introduce to our sons and nephews in America. No one offers us their sons for our daughters.

Mariah lives next door to a famous woman writer in Soweto and offers to carry a letter to her from Kitchen Table: Women of Color Press. Posted mail from abroad so often does not reach its destination in Soweto. Round, quick, and with a brilliant smile, Mariah sits near the top of the Executive Board of Zamani. There is a presence about her of a successful African market woman, sharp, pleasant, outgoing, and awake to every opportunity.

Sofia keeps the books. She is quietly watchful and speaks with that soft humor that is shared by many of the women. She lives and sews alone now that her children are grown and gone away. She likes the way Gloria does her hair, and they discuss different hair preparations. Her eyes are encouraging and attentive as she sits and sews with tiny, rhythmical stitches.

Vibrant young Etta of the beautiful body dances excitement in our frequent spontaneous dancing. She is also learning to run the film cameras. Etta is always laughing and full of frolic, and some of the older women watch her and shake their heads with that particular Black women's look. But mostly they laugh back, because Etta's gaiety is so infectious. Her face turns serious as she discusses what she wants to do with her life back home.

Helen is another one of the young ones, as they are called by everyone else. Their relationship to the other women is clearly one of respect, almost like daughters-in-law. And this is in addition to the warmth and mutual esteem evident between all the women. Helen already moves in a dignified and considered way, but she has twinkling and mischievous eyes and tells me confidentially that she is the naughtiest one of all.

Rita, the last of the young ones, is quiet and small and rather proper. All the "mas" like her a lot, and smile approvingly at her. She is always helpful and soft-voiced, and really enjoys singing religious songs.

Bembe, light-skinned and small-boned, cleans and irons all day and sometimes at night when she is disturbed about something, like their imminent trip home. She is Zulu, like Etta, and loves to dance. Butterfly marks across her cheeks suggest she has lacked vitamins for a long time.

Hannah sings a spirited and humorous song about marriage being a stamping out of a woman's freedom, just like her signature in the marriage register is a stamping out of her own name as written in the book of life. All the other women join in the high-spirited chorus with much laughter. This is one of their favorite songs. Hannah talks about mothers-in-law, and how sometimes when they finally get to have their own way, they take it out on their sons' wives. And by tradition, the daughters-in-law must remain meek and helpful, blowing their lungs out firing the wood braziers and coal stoves for the rest of the family every morning. She tells of her own young self rising at 4:00 a.m., even on the morning after her wedding night, lighting the fire to fix her father-in-law his coffee. But she not only eventually stopped this, she even joined her daughter once in punching out her daughter's philandering husband, caught in the act in his wife's bed.

Mary, the oldest woman in the group, is called Number One. Witty, wise, and soft-spoken, she says love and concern came to her very late in life, once she started to work with Zamani. She is very grateful for the existence of the group, a sentiment that is often expressed by many of the other women in various ways. When we part she kisses me on my lips. "I love you, my sister," she says.

Wassa, round-cheeked and matter-of-fact, talks of her fear of reentry into Johannesburg. "But at least we will be all together," she says, "so if something happens to one of us the others can tell her people." I remember Ellen talking of the horror of hitting Jo'burg alone, and how you never know what the South African police might be planning for you at the airport, nor why.

The night before we part we swim in the pool beneath the sweet evening of the grapevines. "We are naked here in this pool now," Wassa says softly, "and we will be naked when we go back home." We told the women we would carry them in our hearts until we were together again. Everyone is anxious to go back home, despite the fear, despite the uncertainty, despite the dangers.

There is work to be done.

August 12, 1986
NEW YORK CITY

Wonderful news! My liver scan shows both tumors slightly diminished. It feels good to be getting on with my life. I feel vindicated without ever becoming complacent—this is only one victory of a long battle in which I've got to expect to win some and lose some. But it does put a different perspective upon things to know that pain can be a sign of a disintegrating tumor. Of course, my oncologist is surprised and puzzled. He admits he doesn't understand what is happening, but it is a mark of his good spirit that he is genuinely pleased for me, nonetheless. I'm very pleased for me, too.

A good autumn coming, if I remember to take it easily. I have interesting classes, and SISA is planning a benefit this fall around the quilt Gloria and I brought back from the Zamani Soweto Sisters in Europe. I'll be doing another benefit for Kitchen Table in Boston. That feels real good. It will be six years next month since the vision of KTP became a reality through the hard work of Barbara and Cherrie and Myrna and the others.

~

August 15, 1986
NEW YORK CITY

Women of Color in struggle all over the world, our separateness, our connectedness, so many more options for survival. Whatever I call them, I know them for sister, mother, daughter, voice and teacher, inheritor of fire. Alice of Soweto cursing the mission songs: "We have our own political songs now for the young people to sing—no more damn forgiveness!" Her voice is almost hysterically alone in the shocked silence of the other hymn-singing women.

Katerina stands in the Berlin hall, two hours into the discussion that follows the poetry reading by her and other Afro-German women. "I have had enough," she says, "and yes, you may need to continue to air your feelings of racism because for you they are a new discovery here tonight. But I have known them and lived with them all of my life and tonight it is now time for me to go home." And she walks down the aisle and out, straight and beautiful, with that fine and familiar Black woman's audacity in the face of a totally unsupported situation.

Rangitunoa, Maori tribal woman, standing to speak in her people's sacred place, the *marae*. Women have not spoken here before because they have not known the ancient language. In the old days, women did not speak in the *marae* at all. Now this young woman who loves women stands to speak in the tongue of her people, eloquently alone and suspect in her elders' eyes.

Dinah, Aboriginal woman come down from the hot north hills of the outback, traveling by bus three days from mission to mission to meet with the writing women of Melbourne, because she had heard of this conference and she wishes to bring her stories to them.

The stern, shy Samoan women in Auckland, plush and mighty, organizing study groups for their teen-aged kin, holding evening classes for them in how to understand the *Pakahas* (whites).

The Aboriginal women reclaiming the famous Ayers Rock as *Ulluru*, a place of women's Dreaming.

The women of the South Pacific islands demanding their peoples' land rights, rejecting the European and American nuclear madness that is devastating their islands.

Brown people filling the streets of downtown Auckland, marching in support of a Nuclear Free and Independent Pacific. It could almost be Washington, D.C.!

Black children sitting down in the middle of metropolitan Melbourne to celebrate Koori Day, the Black, Red, and Yellow flag of Pacific Liberation and revolution snapping in the sun. "What do we want? LAND RIGHTS! When do we want them? NOW!!" Banners ringing the shopping mall in Black, Red, and Yellow: PAY THE RENT!

Merle, fierce and shining, a Caribbean woman writer calmly analyzing the sexism behind the lyrics of beloved calypsos.

The Black South African seamstresses telling their multifaceted stories of survival, their soft voices filled with what Gloria calls a revolutionary patience.

Black women taking care of business all over the world.

~

September 21, 1986
NEW YORK CITY

The Autumn Equinox, a time of balancing. Nudie died of lung cancer today in Puerto Rico. Frances and I had just come back from a beautiful weekend in Shelter Island, and as we walked in the phone was ringing and it was Yoli. I feel that same sadness and fury as when I heard Hyllus Maris had died in Melbourne last month. Some of us refuse to have anything to do with other people who have cancer, reluctant to invite another sorrow, as if any reflection of our own battle either lessens our power or makes it too realistic to be borne. Others of us fashion a connection of support, but sometimes that connection is not solid enough and invites another grief. I felt I had a special pact with Hyllus and with Nudie. As if we had promised each other we would make it, but nobody does, and they didn't, and I won't either.

But magical thinking doesn't work. I'm so glad Nudie had a chance to go back to Puerto Rico, which is where she always wanted to end up her time.

Making it really means doing it our way for as long as possible, same as crossing a busy avenue or telling unpleasant truths. But even though it's childish and useless, I'm still angry with both of them for dying.

That's probably how some of my friends feel about me right now, the ones who can't look me in the eye when they ask how I'm doing, even though I'm very much alive and kicking.

It's nine years ago today I had my first breast biopsy. Which was outstandingly and conclusively negative. So much for biopsies. Bob Marley weaving through my visualizations:

> won't you help me sing
> these songs of freedom
> was all I ever ha'd
> redemption songs

~

September 27, 1986
NEW YORK CITY

I hope when I reread this journal later there will be more here than simply a record of who died in what month and how their passing touched me. Maybe at least how I can use that knowledge to move beyond the moments of terror. I much prefer to think about how I'd want to die—given that I don't want to die at all but will certainly have to—rather than just fall into death any old way, by default, according to somebody else's rules. It's not like you get a second chance to die the way you want to die.

Sometimes I have the eeriest feeling that I'm living some macabre soap opera. And *too besides,* it's being recorded in vivid living color. If so, I hope it'll be useful someday for something, if only for some other Black sister's afternoon entertainment when her real life gets to be too much. It'll sure beat "As the World Turns." At least there will be real Black people in this one, and maybe if I'm lucky, I'll get to drag the story on interminably for twenty or thirty years like the TV soaps, until the writer dies of old age or the audience loses interest— which is another way of saying they no longer need to discharge the tensions in their lives that lie behind that particular story.

~

November 6, 1986
NEW YORK CITY

Black mother goddess, salt dragon of chaos, Seboulisa, Mawu. Attend me, hold me in your muscular flowering arms, protect me from throwing any part of myself away.

Women who have asked me to set these stories down are asking me for my air to breathe, to use in their future, are courting me back to my life as a warrior. Some offer me their bodies, some their enduring patience, some a separate fire, and still others, only a naked need whose face is all too familiar. It is the need to give voice to the complexities of living with cancer, outside of the tissue-thin assurance that they "got it all," or that the changes we have wrought in our lives will insure that cancer never reoccurs. And it is a need to give voice to living with cancer outside of that numbing acceptance of death as a resignation waiting after fury and before despair.

There is nothing I cannot use somehow in my living and my work, even if I would never have chosen it on my own, even if I am livid with fury at having to choose. Not only did nobody ever say it would be easy, nobody ever said what faces the challenges would wear. The point is to do as much as I can of what I came to do before they nickel and dime me to death.

Racism. Cancer. In both cases, to win the aggressor must conquer, but the resisters need only survive. How do I define that survival and on whose terms?

So I feel a sense of triumph as I pick up my pen and say yes I am going to write again from the world of cancer and with a different perspective—that of living with cancer in an intimate daily relationship. Yes, I'm going to say plainly, six years after my mastectomy, in spite of drastically altered patterns of eating and living, and in spite of my self-conscious living and increased self-empowerment, and in spite of my deepening commitment to using myself in the service of what I believe, and in spite of all my positive expectations to the contrary, I have been diagnosed as having cancer of the liver, metastasized from breast cancer.

This fact does not make my last six years of work any less vital or important or necessary. The accuracy of that diagnosis has become less important than how I use the life I have.

November 8, 1986

If I am to put this all down in a way that is useful, I should start with the beginning of the story.

Sizable tumor in the right lobe of the liver, the doctors said. Lots of blood vessels in it means it's most likely malignant. Let's cut you open right now and see what we can do about it. Wait a minute, I said. I need to feel this thing out and see what's going on inside myself first, I said, needing some time to absorb the shock, time to assay the situation and not act out of panic. Not one of them said, I can respect that, but don't take too long about it.

Instead, that simple claim to my body's own processes elicited such an attack response from a reputable Specialist In Liver Tumors that my deepest—if not necessarily most useful—suspicions were totally aroused.

What that doctor could have said to me that I would have heard was, "You have a serious condition going on in your body and whatever you do about it you must not ignore it or delay deciding how you are going to deal with it because it will not go away no matter what you think it is." Acknowledging my responsibility for my own body. Instead, what he said to me was, "If you do not do exactly what I tell you to do right now without questions you are going to die a horrible death." In exactly those words.

I felt the battle lines being drawn up within my own body.

I saw this specialist in liver tumors at a leading cancer hospital in New York City, where I had been referred as an outpatient by my own doctor.

The first people who interviewed me in white coats from behind a computer were only interested in my health-care benefits and proposed method of payment. Those crucial facts determined what kind of plastic ID card I would be given, and without a plastic ID card, no one at all was allowed upstairs to see any doctor, as I was told by the uniformed, pistoled guards at all the stairwells.

From the moment I was ushered into the doctor's office and he saw my x-rays, he proceeded to infantalize me with an obviously well-practiced technique. When I told him I was having second thoughts about a liver biopsy, he glanced at my chart. Racism and Sexism joined hands across his table as he saw I taught at a university. "Well, you look like an *intelligent girl*," he said, staring at my one breast all the time he was speaking. "Not to have this biopsy immediately is like sticking your head in the sand." Then he went on to say that he would not be responsible when I wound up one day screaming in agony in the corner of his office!

I asked this specialist in liver tumors about the dangers of a liver biopsy spreading an existing malignancy, or even encouraging it in a borderline tumor. He dismissed my concerns with a wave of his hand, saying, instead of answering, that I really did not have any other sensible choice.

I would like to think that this doctor was sincerely motivated by a desire for me to seek what he truly believed to be the only remedy for my sickening body, but my faith in that scenario is considerably diminished by his $250 consultation fee and his subsequent medical report to my own doctor containing numerous supposedly clinical observations of *obese abdomen* and *remaining pendulous breast*.

In any event, I can thank him for the fierce shard lancing through my terror that shrieked there must be some other way, this doesn't feel right to me. If this is cancer and they cut me open to find out, what is stopping that intrusive action from spreading the cancer, or turning a questionable mass into an active malignancy? All I was asking for was the reassurance of a realistic answer to my real questions, and that was not forthcoming. I made up my mind that if I was going to die in agony on somebody's office floor, it certainly wasn't going to be his! I needed information, and pored over books on the liver in Barnes & Noble's Medical Textbook Section on Fifth Avenue for hours. I learned, among other things, that the liver is the largest, most complex, and most generous organ in the human body. But that did not help me very much.

In this period of physical weakness and psychic turmoil, I found myself going through an intricate inventory of rage. First of all at my breast surgeon—had he perhaps done something wrong? How could such a small breast tumor have metastasized? Hadn't he assured me he'd gotten it all, and what was this now anyway about micro-metastases? Could this tumor in my liver have been seeded at the same time as my breast cancer? There were so many unanswered questions, and too much that I just did not understand.

But my worst rage was the rage at myself. For a brief time I felt like a total failure. What had I been busting my ass doing these past six years if it wasn't living and loving and working to my utmost potential? And wasn't that all a guarantee supposed to keep exactly this kind of thing from ever happening again? So what had I done wrong and what was I going to have to pay for it and WHY ME?

But finally a little voice inside me said sharply, "Now really, is there any other way you would have preferred living the past six years that would have been more satisfying? And be that as it may, *should* or *shouldn't* isn't even the question. How do you want to live the rest of your life from now on and what are you going to do about it?" Time's a-wasting!

Gradually, in those hours in the stacks of Barnes & Noble, I felt myself shifting into another gear. My resolve strengthened as my panic lessened. Deep breathing, regularly. I'm not going to let them cut into my body again until I'm convinced there is no other alternative. And this time, the burden of proof rests with the doctors because their record of success with liver cancer is not so good that it would make me jump at a surgical solution. And scare tactics are not going to work. I have been scared now for six years and that hasn't stopped me. I've given myself plenty of practice in doing whatever I need to do, scared or not, so scare tactics are just not going to work. Or I hoped they were not going to work. At any rate, thank the goddess, they were not working yet. One step at a time.

But some of my nightmares were pure hell, and I started having trouble sleeping.

In writing this I have discovered how important some things are that I thought were unimportant. I discovered this by the high price they exact for scrutiny. At first I did not want to look again at how I slowly came to terms with my own mortality on a level deeper than before, nor with the inevitable strength that gave me as I started to get on with my life in actual time. Medical textbooks on the liver were fine, but there were appointments to be kept, and bills to pay, and decisions about my upcoming trip to Europe to be made. And what do I say to my children? Honesty has always been the bottom line between us, but did I really need them going through this with me during their final difficult years at college? On the other hand, how could I shut them out of this most important decision of my life?

I made a visit to my breast surgeon, a doctor with whom I have always been able to talk frankly, and it was from him that I got my first trustworthy and objective sense of timing. It was from him that I learned that the conventional forms of treatment for liver metastases made little more than one year's difference in the survival rate. I heard my old friend Clem's voice coming back to me through the dimness of thirty years: "I see you coming here trying to make sense where there is no sense. Try just living in it. Respond, alter, see what happens." I thought of the African way of perceiving life, as experience to be lived rather than as problem to be solved.

Homeopathic medicine calls cancer the cold disease. I understand that down to my bones that quake sometimes in their need for heat, for the sun, even for just a hot bath. Part of the way in which I am saving my own life is to refuse to submit my body to cold whenever possible.

In general, I fight hard to keep my treatment scene together in some coherent and serviceable way, integrated into my daily living and absolute. Forgetting is no excuse. It's as simple as one missed shot could make the difference between a quiescent malignancy and one that is growing again. This not only keeps me in an intimate, positive relationship to my own health, but it also underlines the fact that I have the responsibility for attending my own health. I cannot simply hand over that responsibility to anybody else.

Which does not mean I give in to the belief, arrogant or naive, that I know everything I need to know in order to make informed decisions about my body. But attending my own health, gaining enough information to help me understand and participate in the decisions made about my body by people who know more medicine than I do, are all crucial strategies in my battle for living. They also provide me with important prototypes for doing battle in all other arenas of my life.

Battling racism and battling heterosexism and battling apartheid share the same urgency inside me as battling cancer. None of these struggles are ever easy, and even the smallest victory is never to be taken for granted. Each victory must be applauded, because it is so easy not to battle at all, to just accept and call that acceptance inevitable.

And all power is relative. Recognizing the existence as well as the limitations of my own power, and accepting the responsibility for using it in my own behalf, involve me in direct and daily actions that preclude denial as a possible refuge. Simone de Beauvoir's words echo in my head: "It is in the recognition of the genuine conditions of our lives that we gain the strength to act and our motivation for change."

~

November 10, 1986
NEW YORK CITY

Building into my living—without succumbing to it—an awareness of this reality of my life, that I have a condition within my body of which I will eventually die, comes in waves, like a rising tide. It exists side by side with another force inside me that says no you don't, not you, and the x-rays are wrong and the tests are wrong and the doctors are wrong.

There is a different kind of energy inherent within each one of these feelings, and I try to reconcile and use these different energies whenever I need them. The energy generated by the first awareness serves to urge me always to get on with living my life and doing my work with an intensity and purpose of the urgent now. Throw the toys overboard, we're headed into rougher waters.

The energies generated by the second force fuel a feisty determination to continue doing what I am doing forever. The tensions created inside me by the contradictions is another source of energy and learning. I have always known I learn my most lasting lessons about difference by closely attending the ways in which the differences inside me lie down together.

~

November 11, 1986
NEW YORK CITY

I keep observing how other people die, comparing, learning, critiquing the process inside of me, matching it up to how I would like to do it. And I think about this scrutiny of myself in the context of its usefulness to other Black women living with cancer, born and unborn.

I have a privileged life or else I would be dead by now. It is two and a half years since the first tumor in my liver was discovered. When I needed to know, there was no one around to tell me that there were alternatives to turning myself over to doctors who are terrified of not knowing everything. There was no one around to remind me that I have a right to decide what happens to my own body, not because I know more than anybody else, but simply because it is my body. And I have a right to acquire the information that can help me make those crucial decisions.

It was an accident of circumstance that brought me to Germany at a critical moment in my health, and another which introduced me to one holistic/homeopathic approach to the treatment of certain cancers. Not all homeopathic alternatives work for every patient. Time is a crucial element in the treatment of cancer, and I had to decide which chances I would take, and why.

I think of what this means to other Black women living with cancer, to all women in general. Most of all I think of how important it is for us to share with each other the powers buried within the breaking of silence about our bodies and our health, even though we have been schooled to be secret and stoical about pain and disease. But that stoicism and silence does not serve us nor our communities, only the forces of things as they are.

~

November 12, 1986
NEW YORK CITY

When I write my own Book of the Dead, my own Book of Life, I want to celebrate being alive to do it even while I acknowledge the painful savor uncertainty lends to my living. I use the energy of dreams that are now impossible, not totally believing in them nor their power to become real, but recognizing them as templates for a future within which my labors can play a part. I am freer to choose what I will devote my energies toward and what I will leave for another lifetime, thanking the goddess for the strength to perceive that I can choose, despite obstacles.

So when I do a SISA reading to raise funds for the women's collectives in Soweto, or to raise money for Kitchen Table: Women of Color Press, I am choosing to use myself for things in which I passionately believe. When I speak to rally support in the urgent war against apartheid in South Africa and the racial slaughter that is even now spreading across the U.S., when I demand justice in the police shotgun killing of a Black grandmother and lynchings in Northern California and in Central Park in New York City, I am making a choice of how I wish to use my power. This work gives me a tremendous amount of energy back in satisfaction and in belief, as well as in a vision of how I want this earth to be for the people who come after me.

When I work with young poets who are reaching for the power of their poetry within themselves and the lives they choose to live, I feel I am working to capacity, and this gives me deep joy, a reservoir of strength I draw upon for the next venture. Right now. This makes it far less important that it will not be forever. It never was.

The energies I gain from my work help me neutralize those implanted forces of negativity and self-destructiveness that is white America's way of making sure I keep whatever is powerful and creative within me unavailable, ineffective, and nonthreatening.

But there is a terrible clarity that comes from living with cancer that can be empowering if we do not turn aside from it. What more can they do to me? My time is limited, and this is so for each one of us. So how will the opposition reward me for my silences? For the pretense that this is in fact the best of all possible worlds? What will they give me for lying? A lifelong Safe-Conduct Pass for everyone I love? Another lifetime for me? The end to racism? Sexism? Homophobia? Cruelty? The common cold?

~

November 13, 1986
NEW YORK CITY

I do not find it useful any longer to speculate upon cancer as a political weapon. But I'm not being paranoid when I say my cancer is as political as if some CIA agent brushed past me in the A train on March 15, 1965 and air-injected me with a long-fused cancer virus. Or even if it is only that I stood in their wind to do my work and the billows flayed me. What possible choices do most of us have in the air we breathe and the water we must drink?

Sometimes we are blessed with being able to choose the time and the arena and the manner of our revolution, but more usually we must do battle wherever we are standing. It does not matter too much if it is in the radiation lab or a doctor's office or the telephone company, the streets, the welfare department, or the classroom. The real blessing is to be able to use whoever I am wherever I am, in concert with as many others as possible, or alone if needs be.

This is no longer a time of waiting. It is a time for the real work's urgencies. It is a time enhanced by an iron reclamation of what I call the burst of light—that inescapable knowledge, in the bone, of my own physical limitation. Metabolized and integrated into the fabric of my days, that knowledge makes the particulars of what is coming seem less important. When I speak of wanting as much good time as possible, I mean time over which I maintain some relative measure of control.

~

November 14, 1986
New York City

One reason I watch the death process so acutely is to rob it of some of its power over my consciousness. I have overcome my earlier need to ignore or turn away from films and books that deal with cancer or dying. It is ever so much more important now for me to fill the psyches of all the people I love and who love me with a sense of outrageous beauty and strength of purpose.

But it is also true that sometimes we cannot heal ourselves close to the very people from whom we draw strength and light, because they are also closest to the places and tastes and smells that go along with a pattern of living we are trying to rearrange. After my mastectomy, changing the ways I ate and struggled and slept and meditated also required that I change the external environment within which I was deciding what direction I would have to take.

I am on the cusp of change and the curve is shifting fast. If any of my decisions have been in error, I must stand—not prepared, for that is impossible—but open to dealing with the consequences of those errors.

Inside and outside, change is not easy nor quick, and I find myself always on guard against what is oversimplified, or merely cosmetic.

~

November 15, 1986
New York City

In my office at home I have created a space that is very special to me. It is simple and quiet, with beautiful things about, and a ray of sunlight cascading through a low window on the best of days. It is here that I write whenever I am home, and where I retreat to center myself, to rest and recharge at regular intervals. It is here that I do my morning visualizations and my eurhythmics.

It is a tiny alcove with an air mattress half-covered with bright pillows, and a low narrow table with a Nigerian tie-dye throw. Against one wall and central to this space is a painting by a young Guyanese woman called *The Yard*. It is a place of water and fire and flowers

118 888888

and trees, filled with Caribbean women and children working and playing and being.

When the sun lances through my small window and touches the painting, the yard comes alive. The red spirit who lives at the center of the painting flames. Children laugh, a woman nurses her baby, a little naked boy cuts the grass. One woman is building a fire outside for cooking; inside a house another woman is fixing a light. In a slat-house up the hill, windows are glowing under the red-tiled roof.

I keep company with the women of this place.

Yesterday, I sat in this space with a sharp Black woman, discussing the focus of a proposed piece for a Black women's magazine. We talked about whether it should be about the role of art and spirituality in Black women's lives, or about my survival struggles with current bouts of cancer. As we talked, I gradually realized that both articles were grounded in the same place within me, and required the same focus. I require the nourishment of art and spirituality in my life, and they lend strength and insight to all the endeavors that give substance to my living. It is the bread of art and the water of my spiritual life that remind me always to reach for what is highest within my capacities and in my demands of myself and others. Not for what is perfect but for what is the best possible. And I orchestrate my daily anticancer campaign with an intensity intrinsic to who I am, the intensity of making a poem. It is the same intensity with which I experience poetry, a student's first breakthrough, the loving energy of women I do not even know, the posted photograph of a sunrise taken from my winter dawn window, the intensity of loving.

I revel in the beauty of the faces of Black women at labor and at rest. I make, demand, translate satisfactions out of every ray of sunlight, scrap of bright cloth, beautiful sound, delicious smell that comes my way, out of every sincere smile and good wish. They are discreet bits of ammunition in my arsenal against despair. They all contribute to the strengthening of my determination to persevere when the greyness overwhelms, or Reaganomics wears me down. They whisper to me of joy when the light is dim, when I falter, when another Black child is gunned down from behind in Crossroads or Newark or lynched from a tree in Memphis, and when the health orchestration gets boring or depressing or just plain too much.

~

November 16, 1986
NEW YORK CITY

For Black women, learning to consciously extend ourselves to each other and to call upon each other's strengths is a life-saving strategy. In the best of circumstances surrounding our lives, it requires an enormous amount of mutual, consistent support for us to be emotionally able to look straight into the face of the powers aligned against us and still do our work with joy.

It takes determination and practice.

Black women who survive have a head start in learning how to be open and self-protective at the same time. One secret is to ask as many people as possible for help, depending on all of them and on none of them at the same time. Some will help, others cannot. For the time being.

Another secret is to find some particular thing your soul craves for nourishment—a different religion, a quiet spot, a dance class—and satisfy it. That satisfaction does not have to be costly or difficult. Only a need that is recognized, articulated, and answered.

There is an important difference between openness and naiveté. Not everyone has good intentions nor means me well. I remind myself I do not need to change these people, only recognize who they are.

~

November 17, 1986
NEW YORK CITY

How has everyday living changed for me with the advent of a second cancer? I move through a terrible and invigorating savor of now—a visceral awareness of the passage of time, with its nightmare and its energy. No more long-term loans, extended payments, twenty-year plans. Pay my debts. Call the tickets in, the charges, the emotional IOU's. Now is the time, if ever, once and for all, to alter the patterns of isolation. Remember that nice lady down the street whose son you used to cross at the light and who was always saying, "Now if there's ever anything I can do for you, just let me know." Well, her boy's got strong muscles and the lawn needs mowing.

I am not ashamed to let my friends know I need their collective spirit—not to make me live forever, but rather to help me move through the life I have. But I refuse to spend the rest of that life mourning what I do not have.

If living as a poet—living on the front lines—has ever had meaning, it has meaning now. Living a self-conscious life, vulnerability as armor.

I spend time every day meditating upon my physical self in battle, visualizing the actual war going on inside my body. As I move through the other parts of each day, that battle often merges with particular external campaigns, both political and personal. The devastations of apartheid in South Africa and racial murder in Howard Beach feel as critical to me as cancer.

Among my other daily activities I incorporate brief periods of physical self-monitoring without hysteria. I attend the changes within my body, anointing myself with healing light. Sometimes I have to do it while sitting on the Staten Island Ferry on my way home, surrounded by snapping gum and dirty rubber boots, all of which I banish from my consciousness.

I am learning to reduce stress in my practical everyday living. It's nonsense, however, to believe that any Black woman who is living an informed life in America can possibly abolish stress totally from her life without becoming psychically deaf, mute, and blind. *(News Item: Unidentified Black man found hanging from a tree in Central Park with hands and feet bound. New York City police call it a suicide.)* I am learning to balance stress with periods of rest and restoration.

I juggle the technologies of eastern medicine with the holistic approach of anthroposophy with the richness of my psychic life, beautifully and womanfully nourished by people I love and who love me. Balancing them all. Knowing over and over again how blessed I am in my life, my loves, my children; how blessed I am in being able to give myself to work in which I passionately believe. And yes, some days I wish to heaven to Mawu to Seboulisa to Tiamat daughter of chaos that it could all have been easier.

But I wake in an early morning to see the sun rise over the tenements of Brooklyn across the bay, fingering through the wintered arms of the raintree Frances and I planted as a thin stick seventeen years ago, and I cannot possibly imagine trading my life for anyone else's, no matter how near termination that life may be. Living fully—how long is not the point. How and why take total precedence.

~

November 18, 1986
NEW YORK CITY

Despair and isolation are my greatest internal enemies. I need to remember I am not alone, even when it feels that way. Now more than ever it is time to put my solitary ways behind me, even while protecting my solitude. "Help is on the way," Margareta said, her fingers moving over the Tarot deck in a farewell gesture.

I need to identify that help and use it whenever I can.

Five million people in the U.S.—or two percent of the population of this country—are actively living with cancer. If you apply that percentage to the Black community—where it is probably higher because of the rising incidence of cancers without a corresponding rise in the cure rate—if we take that percentage into the Black population of 22 million, then every single day there are at least half a million Black people in the U.S. shopping in supermarkets, catching subways, grooming mules, objecting in PTA meetings, standing in a welfare line, teaching Sunday school, walking in the streets at noon looking for work, scrubbing a kitchen floor, all carrying within our bodies the seeds of a destruction not of our own choosing. It is a destruction we can keep from defining our living for as long as possible, if not our dying. Each one of us must define for ourselves what substance and shape we wish to give the life we have left.

~

November 19, 1986
NEW YORK CITY

Evil never appears in its own face to bargain, nor does impotence, nor does despair. After all, who believes anymore in the devil buying up souls, anyway? But I warn myself, don't even pretend not to say no, loudly and often, no matter how symbolically. Because the choices presented in our lives are never simple or fable-clear. Survival never presents itself as "do this particular thing precisely as directed and you will go on living. Don't do that and no question about it you will surely die." Despite what the doctor said, it just doesn't happen that way.

Probably in some ideal world we would be offered distinct choices, where we make our decisions from a clearly typed and annotated menu. But no life for any Black woman I know is that simple or that banal. There are as many crucial, untimed decisions to be made as there are dots in a newspaper photo of great contrast, and as we get close enough to examine them within their own terrain, the whole picture becomes distorted and obscure.

I do not think about my death as being imminent, but I live my days against a background noise of mortality and constant uncertainty. Learning not to crumple before these uncertainties fuels my resolve to print myself upon the texture of each day fully rather than forever.

December 1, 1986
NEW YORK CITY

Cancer survivors are expected to be silent out of misguided concerns for others' feelings of guilt or despair, or out of a belief in the myth that there can be self-protection through secrecy. By and large, outside the radiation lab or the doctor's office, we are invisible to each other, and we begin to be invisible to ourselves. We begin to doubt whatever power we once knew we had, and once we doubt our power, we stop using it. We rob our comrades, our lovers, our friends, and our selves of ourselves.

I have periods of persistent and distracting visceral discomfort that are totally intrusive and energy-consuming. I say this rather than simply use the word *pain,* because there are too many gradations of effect and response that are not covered by that one word. Self-hypnosis seemed a workable possibility for maintaining some control over the processes going on inside my body. With trial and inquiry, I found a reliable person to train me in the techniques of self-hypnosis. It's certainly cheaper than codeine.

Self-hypnosis requires a concentration so intense I put myself into a waking trance. But we go into those states more often than we realize. Have you ever been wide awake on the subway and missed your station because you were thinking about something else? It's a question of recognizing this state and learning to use it to manipulate my consciousness of pain.

One of the worst things about intrusive pain is that it makes me feel impotent, unable to move against it and therefore against anything else, as if the pain swallows up all ability to act. Self-hypnosis has been useful to me not only for refocusing physical discomfort, it has also been useful to me in helping effect other bargains with my unconscious self. I've been able to use it to help me remember my dreams, raise a subnormal body temperature, and bring myself to complete a difficult article.

I respect the time I spend each day treating my body, and I consider it part of my political work. It is possible to have some conscious input into our physical processes—not expecting the impossible, but allowing for the unexpected—a kind of training in self-love and physical resistance.

~

December 7, 1986
NEW YORK CITY

I'm glad I don't have to turn away any more from movies about people dying of cancer. I no longer have to deny cancer as a reality in my life. As I wept over *Terms of Endearment* last night, I also laughed. It's hard to believe I avoided this movie for over two years.

Yet while I was watching it, involved in the situation of a young mother dying of breast cancer, I was also very aware of that standard of living, taken for granted in the film, that made the expression of her tragedy possible. Her mother's maid and the manicured garden, the unremarked but very tangible money so evident through its effects. Daughter's philandering husband is an unsuccessful English professor, but they still live in a white-shingled house with trees, not in some rack-ass tenement on the Lower East Side or in Harlem for which they pay too much rent.

Her private room in Lincoln Memorial Hospital has her mama's Renoir on the wall. There are never any Black people at all visible in that hospital in Lincoln, Nebraska, not even in the background. Now this may not make her death scenes any less touching, but it did strengthen my resolve to talk about my experiences with cancer as a Black woman.

December 14, 1986

NEW YORK CITY

It is exactly one year since I went to Switzerland and found the air cold and still. Yet what I found at the Lukas Klinik has helped me save my life.

~

December 15, 1986

NEW YORK CITY

To acknowledge privilege is the first step in making it available for wider use. Each of us is blessed in some particular way, whether we recognize our blessings or not. And each one of us, somewhere in our lives, must clear a space within that blessing where she can call upon whatever resources are available to her in the name of something that must be done.

I have been very blessed in my life. I have been blessed to believe passionately, to love deeply, and to be able to work out of those loves and beliefs. Accidents of privilege allowed me to gain information about holistic/biological medicine and their approach to cancers, and that information has helped keep me alive, along with my original gut feeling that said, *Stay out of my body.* For me, living and the use of that living are inseparable, and I have a responsibility to put that privilege and that life to use.

For me, living fully means living with maximum access to my experience and power, loving, and doing work in which I believe. It means writing my poems, telling my stories, and speaking out of my most urgent concerns and against the many forms of anti-life surrounding us.

I wish to live whatever life I have as fully and as sweetly as possible, rather than refocus that life solely upon extending it for some unspecified time. I consider this a political decision as well as a life-saving one, and it is a decision that I am fortunate to be able to make.

If one Black woman I do not know gains hope and strength from my story, then it has been worth the difficulty of telling.

~

Epilogue

Sometimes I feel like I am living on a different star from the one I am used to calling home. It has not been a steady progression. I had to examine, in my dreams as well as in my immune-function tests, the devastating effects of overextension. Overextending myself is not stretching myself. I had to accept how difficult it is to monitor the difference. Necessary for me as cutting down on sugar. Crucial. Physically. Psychically. Caring for myself is not self-indulgence, it is self-preservation, and that is an act of political warfare.

Time in this place is speedy, rich, and stark. My days are a thirsty atonal combination of the mundane and the apocalyptic. Mingling without much warming. Moving without missing a beat from the report of peritubal metastases (Does that mean escape into the abdominal cavity?) to estimates for constructing my workspace in St. Croix. Drastic life-changes laced together with the eternal ordinary.

My aim is to move more easily between the two, make transitions the least costly, approach a student's completed manuscript and the medical reports

and the house estimates in some open-hearted way, with a sense of propor-
tion. I order a perfume from Grenada called "Jump Up and Kiss Me."

I try to weave my life-prolonging treatments into a living context—
to resist giving myself over like a sacrificial offering to the furious
single-minded concentration upon cure that leaves no room to examine
what living and fighting on a physical front can mean. What living with can-
cer can teach me. I go to Germany this fall for further mistletoe treatment.
I look forward to working again with the Afro-German Women's Group.

I believe that one of the ways in which cancer cells insure their own
life and depress the immune system is by creating a physiologically
engendered despair. Learning to fight that despair in all its manifesta-
tions is not only therapeutic. It is vital. Underlining what is joyful and
life-affirming in my living becomes crucial.

What have I had to leave behind? Old life habits, outgrown defenses
put aside lest they siphon off energies to no useful purpose?

One of the hardest things to accept is learning to live within uncertainty
and neither deny it nor hide behind it. Most of all, to listen to the messages
of uncertainty without allowing them to immobilize me, nor keep me from
the certainties of those truths in which I believe. I turn away from any need
to justify the future—to live in what has not yet been. Believing, working
for what has not yet been while living fully in the present now.

This is my life. Each hour is a possibility not to be banked. These
days are not a preparation for living, some necessary but essentially
extraneous divergence from the main course of my living. They are
my life. The feeling of the bedsheet against my heels as I wake to the
sound of crickets and bananaquits in Judith's Fancy. I am living my life
every particular day no matter where I am, nor in what pursuit. It is
the consciousness of this that gives a marvelous breadth to everything

I do consciously. My most deeply held convictions and beliefs can be equally expressed in how I deal with chemotherapy as well as in how I scrutinize a poem. It's about trying to know who I am wherever I am. It's not as if I'm in struggle over here while someplace else, over there, real life is waiting for me to begin living it again.

I visualize daily winning the battles going on inside my body, and this is an important part of fighting for my life. In those visualizations, the cancer at times takes on the face and shape of my most implacable enemies, those I fight and resist most fiercely. Sometimes the wanton cells in my liver become Bull Connor and his police dogs completely smothered, rendered impotent in Birmingham, Alabama by a mighty avalanche of young, determined Black marchers moving across him toward their future. P.W. Botha's bloated face of apartheid squashed into the earth beneath an onslaught of the slow rhythmic advance of furious Blackness. Black South African women moving through my blood destroying passbooks. Fireburn Mary* sweeping over the Cruzan countryside, axe and torch in hand. Images from a Calypso singer:

> The big black boot of freedom
> Is mashing down your doorstep.

I train myself for triumph by knowing it is mine, no matter what. In fact, I am surrounded within my external living by ample examples of the struggle for life going on inside me. Visualizing the disease process inside my body in political images is not a quixotic dream. When I speak out against the cynical U.S. intervention in Central America, I am working to save my life in every sense. Government research grants to the National Cancer Institute were cut in 1986 by

---

* Ex-slave who led a workers' revolt in St. Croix in 1848.

the exact amount illegally turned over to the contras in Nicaragua. One hundred and five million dollars. It gives yet another meaning to the personal as the political.

Cancer itself has an anonymous face. When we are visibly dying of cancer, it is sometimes easier to turn away from the particular experience into the sadness of loss, and when we are surviving, it is sometimes easier to deny that experience. But those of us who live our battles in the flesh must know ourselves as our strongest weapon in the most gallant struggle of our lives.

Living with cancer has forced me to consciously jettison the myth of omnipotence, of believing—or loosely asserting—that I can do anything, along with any dangerous illusion of immortality. Neither of these unscrutinized defenses is a solid base for either political activism or personal struggle. But in their place, another kind of power is growing, tempered and enduring, grounded within the realities of what I am in fact doing. An open-eyed assessment and appreciation of what I can and do accomplish, using who I am and who I most wish myself to be. To stretch as far as I can go and relish what is satisfying rather than what is sad. Building a strong and elegant pathway toward transition.

I work, I love, I rest, I see and learn. And I report. These are my givens. Not sureties, but a firm belief that whether or not living them with joy prolongs my life, it certainly enables me to pursue the objectives of that life with a deeper and more effective clarity.

August 1987
Carriacou, Grenada
Anguilla, British West Indies
St. Croix, Virgin Islands